The Fine Art of
QUILTING

The Fine Art of
QUILTING

Vicki Barker · Tessa Bird

E. P. DUTTON NEW YORK

First published in the United States, 1988, by E. P. Dutton, a division of NAL Penguin Inc., 2 Park Avenue, New York, N.Y. 10016

Library of Congress Catalog Card Number: 88-71791

ISBN: 0-525-24676-2 (cloth)
ISBN: 0-525-48391-8 (DP)

Design: Caroline Reeves

10 9 8 7 6 5 4 3 2 1

First American Edition

812829

To our mothers,
THERESA and NORMA

CONTENTS

INTRODUCTION

This book is about quilts that express ideas, emotions, colour, form and individuality. It is about the creativity and motivation of the quiltmakers and the techniques they have adopted and developed.

There is nothing known about the woman who made the "Pineapple" quilt illustrated here. The evidence of her life is in the quilt, a strong and intuitive design using recycled fabrics from old clothes. It suggests a harsh life in which an individual's creativity came second to the practical need for survival. Yet it has united both aspects. Women still do this, just as they have always done.

In contrast to the anonymity of the past we have chosen to interview 13 contemporary quilters about the development of their work. From a shared history of quilting, the contemporary work illustrated shows the many different paths that have been taken. We have included women from northern Europe, Australia, and the United States. We also include illustrations of another 35 quilters' work with their comments.

The past ten years have seen the development of the "art" quilt. Many quilters, no longer content to be constrained by the traditional structures, have experimented with the quilt form as a way of expressing ideas and emotions. As quilts have become statements of individual interests, so their domestic function has become less significant.

It is interesting to find that many contemporary quilters have had art training, studying both fine arts and crafts. They are drawing on the history of painting, ceramics, illustration and graphics, and much of their work

contains references outside those of traditional patchwork. But they come to fabric and quilting because it best suits them as a means of expression. Why is this? Perhaps because fabric is so familiar. Almost all women learn at some point to sew. As Sabine du Tertre says, "Women are constantly surrounded by linen and clothing." All speak of the appeal of quilts, the softness, their density, the texture of the fabric and the "wrap-aroundness".

Some who started as painters found it difficult to continue while bringing up small children. Painting requires solitary time and solitary thought, whereas quilting, according to Therese May, is "something you can be interrupted at". As the early "Crazy Quilt" shows, quilting offers a way of uniting a domestic life with a creative life. Dinah Prentice talks about the fractured nature of women's lives and of quilts representing a way of bringing the different aspects together. Quilts frequently played a part in rites of passage, such as marriage quilts. Joan Schulze's marriage quilt for her son draws on this tradition.

It is sometimes difficult to see the relationship between contemporary and traditional quilts, but there are firm links in both subject matter and techniques. Gardens and flowers feature as strongly now as they have before. From painting and embroidery to the actual caring for gardens, flowers have always been considered an acceptable subject for women. Blocks such as "Ohio Rose" and "Carolina Lily" are standard patterns, graphic depictions, forming a "library" for all to use. The aim of many quilters today is towards a freer use of the quilt form with which to capture impressions and ideas, as in the work of Susan Bartels and Brigitte Fiss.

The interpretation of the environment, both natural and man made, has formed patterns for many traditional blocks, such as ''Moon Over the Mountain'' or ''Log Cabin''. Contemporary quilts combine graphic interpretation with personal beliefs, judgments and social comment,

Below: Anonymous ''Pineapple'' design quilt. (Victoria and Albert Museum).

for example in Dinah Prentice's powerful "Molesworth Mon Amour" and Sonya Lee Barrington's "If you drink, don't drive".

Purely abstract work has always been part of quilting. Amish quilts, produced from the early 18th century in the north-eastern states of America, are highly regarded. Their bold use of colour and simple geometry provide a strong influence for many quilters. Pam Dempster's "Windsail" acknowledges these quilts in design and construction. Rebecca Shore's "Crazy Tile 1" continues another abstract tradition, that of the "Crazy Quilt", one of the earliest types made, by joining together many irregular pieces of material.

Most quilters talk about the necessity of accomplishing traditional sewing techniques first of all, which form the basis of their work. Then they can go on to incorporate new techniques and to experiment with very individual imagery. Sylvia Zumbach, Esther Barrett and Helen Bitar have all constructed quilts using the block form. Pauline Burbidge, Inge Hueber and others use the traditional methods of strip and seminole piecing. Unlike the history of painting, which to many artists can seem daunting, contemporary quilters happily describe themselves as part of a

Above: "Crazy Tile I",
4'9½" × 5'10½"
(1.46 × 1.79m), 1984. Rebecca Shore reveals her delight with fabrics in this quilt, in which many irregular pieces are used in a "crazy" fashion.

tradition and a continuation of it. But the presence of Joan Schulze's work, exhibited in 1986 in Chicago alongside the work of Louise Nevelson, the contemporary American sculptress, indicates that quiltmakers are now being given the status and recognition they have long deserved.

While many quilters continue to make traditional pieces, using the vast range of beautiful blocks and patterns, others are moving further and further in the direction of individual innovation. Therese May's quilt paintings, Barbara Harrow's "moving sculptures" and Jo Budd's "fabric pictures" all represent the diversity of contemporary quilts.

Below: "Snow, Sun, Shadow", 7' × 7' (2.1 × 2.1m), 1986, by Jo Budd.

JOAN SCHULZE, California, USA

Joan Schulze trained as a schoolteacher. After moving to California in 1967, she became involved in embroidery, making her first quilt in 1974. She is now a professional quiltmaker and has exhibited widely throughout the United States and Japan. She teaches and lectures.

I was born and raised in Chicago, in a really tough neighbourhood. I had free rein in the city, walking the streets, down elegant Michigan Avenue or in the poor neighbourhoods, with their fire escapes, big buildings, people walking fast; then there were the famous department stores, Marshall Field's and Carson Pirie Scott's. From the age of about seven I was drawn to the Art Institute of Chicago, where a favourite painting was *A Sunday Afternoon on the Island of La Grande Jatte* by Georges Seurat. I went so often to the Field Museum the museum guards knew me. Among the exhibits was Buckminster Fuller's geodesic dome in mirrors. I used to watch all the people as they were reflected off the hexagons. These two places, I think, formed all of my ideas about exhibiting works of art to the public. They were magical.

When I was 13, in my last year in elementary school, we did costumes for Hallowe'en. I had read a book called *The Patchwork Quilt*. My mother said I could rummage in the rag bag and do whatever I wanted with what was in there. I remember cutting squares. I didn't know how to sew, so I just did big stitches holding all these squares together, and I made a great big pillowcase. I put it on and walked to school, but no one could figure out what I was. I said I was a patchwork quilt. We had no quilt history in our family, and at that time I had never seen one.

In 1967 I moved to California and became involved in stitchery. In 1971 I met Constance Howard, former head of the Textile Department of Goldsmith's College in London. That's when I decided that I would make a commitment and become a professional artist, mainly because she was interested enough in my work to put it in her book *Embroidery and Colour*. I never called myself an "embroideress" or a "stitcher"; I always said "artist".

I wanted to show in New York some day – a really preposterous idea! I was doing wall hangings: very childlike scenes with round suns and hills – all very definable. People liked them. Then I started becoming abstract and very experimental. I'd learn any new technique that came along.

At that time I was looking at things that I knew. I was an elementary school teacher and was looking at illustrations in books – what pleases children, things for the family. Then, little by little, I started going to shows, absorbing different things, and pretty soon I became more adventurous. Only recently my mother said that I always talked about being an artist. But coming from my kind of background, I wouldn't have been able to make a living out of it and I think I sublimated my ambition. I went into teaching because I knew I could always be hired and I thought I could be good at it. I am glad now that I made this decision. Facing

Right: Joan Schulze's studio, a well-organized space for work and reflection. A quilt is in the process of being made.

35 children every day has trained me to think nothing of speaking in public, and to be very organized.

The first quilt I made tied in with the American bicentennial in 1976. I had been teaching quilt techniques, which I had learnt as separate entities, to work into stitchery. In about 1974 people started asking me what kind of quilt I was going to make for the bicentennial. I said, "I'm not a quiltmaker." I felt that quilts were rather ordinary objects – covers for beds, constant repetition and not a lot of fun.

I was then offered a job teaching quiltmaking in the Adult Educa-tion Programme, and had six months to get things together. I hadn't even made a quilt yet! I decided that before I faced this class I should have made one. I don't like to make things unless they are of some use to me, either spiritually, or as gifts. I have four children and my oldest was going to be 12. I started remembering how I had felt when I was nearly 12, and realized that in my own mind I had said that 12 was the end of my childhood. I thought that I would make Derk a quilt. It

would be good for me to practise all the things I was planning to teach, and also to think about his stage in life and what I wanted to say to him. I was anticipating the horrible teenage years ahead. I was concerned also about putting my ideas into this quilt. The funny part was that he was the type of child who never stayed in bed at night. He would always roll off and we would find him on the floor. From the time he put that quilt on, he slept through the night and never fell out of bed again. He has told me how he felt about getting that quilt. It was so special and so different. He has always loved it. Then I realized I would have to make a quilt for each of my children!

At this time I had more space to work in and I wanted my ideas to be larger. I found I couldn't simply translate a small drawing into something big, so I learnt to im-provise even more. I love that big scale; it is very liberating.

In the meantime I had started the Adult Education Programme, which meant dealing with other people's expectations as to what quilts are. My method was totally different from any other teacher at that time because I didn't have a quilt history. We did techniques. We made a group quilt and everybody brought fabric to share. We cut out different sizes and we put them eccentrically together until we saw how we could seam them. That is how I worked out how to be spontaneous! I never started with traditional patterns.

I look at traditional work in a very different way now. I came to use the block, as such, when I did my second quilt for my daughter Dustyne. I appliquéd and embroidered different semi-representational trees and flowers on to fabric rectangles. Then I put them together with fabric strips. Even then I didn't want to do a whole series of the same block.

I did two bicentennial quilts. The first was a big stitchery scene and the second broke away from that and became more pieced. After those two I began to think of California and at that time California meant stars and flowers to me, and hills. I thought I would celebrate California. That's when I started to mix landscape with pattern. I did not realize that no one had ever done this before. I thought it was a fun thing to do, and technically challenging. I could use my batik, dyeing, piecing, and a block and yet still make it into a quilt. It wasn't until a few years later that some people wrote to say they had never seen anything like it.

I don't set out to challenge things, I just have an idea and figure out how to make it visual. I think my eclectic stitchery background has helped me. I use painting, dyeing, piecing, transfer, cutting up, repositioning, and all those things. It's very spontaneous. I know what I want the quilt to look like, but don't have a very clear image until I've actually finished. Now, I have reached a point where I don't have to think about how to make a piece. I can concentrate on images and content.

When I was growing up I never looked at the sky and was not aware of landscape. I was aware of cityscape, sidewalks, buildings and so on. It wasn't until I moved to California that I suddenly started looking at mountains, at sky, stars, rivers, and ocean, and it was a turning point for me.

My visit to Australia has influenced my work. I went on cloud searches! I drove miles and miles and miles through red dust and minimal scenery in the Northern Territory. It's red, red, red, red, plus blue, blue, blue sky. Not many clouds. It's absolutely magnificent. It seeped into me. Then, above Hobart in Tasmania, in the early morning, Mount Wellington turned crimson. That is the colour that is in the two quilts I did to honour my mother and my father.

The last month that I was in Australia I got a phone call to say that my father was dying. When I returned to California I rushed to see him. We had some conversations. It was Christmas time and I had a show in New York. The gallery had sold a piece out of this very special show and I had to make another quilt for them. I was also waiting for the phone call to say my father was dead. I had to focus on something so I didn't fall apart. I made a little quilt. It was a dark and gloomy piece, with a few bright spots. In no way did it relate to my father. It was all the negative stuff that I was trying to offload. The gallery liked it. It was gone for two months and when it came back I was shocked. I had no idea it was such a deadly and claustrophobic piece. The ideas had just flowed through. I could not have done it any other way.

Above: "Conversations with my Father", 3'9" × 6' (1.14 × 1.83m), 1985.

Above: "Poem for my Mother", 3'9" × 6' (1.14 × 1.83m), 1985.

I don't intellectualize my work. Whenever I have, the result has been very dull, very boring – not me at all. It is not that there is no content to the work. There is no life to it, no spontaneity, no feeling of joy. That is the difference.

With the conversations with my father running over and over in my mind, I started painting fabric. He had told me what he was going to see when he went on his journey. He had ideas that he would meet the Indians and talk with them. He was going to flow freely. There'd be no pain. It was a happy

Above: "Free Flight", 7'4" × 6'10" (2.24 × 2.08 m), 1985.

place. We made jokes during those last three days. I said to him that he was going to run through the clouds. So that's what I tried to put into the quilt and I called it "Conversations with my Father".

In "Poem for my Mother" I wanted to tell her how much I really cared about her and what I thought about her life. There are the two eras in her life, youth and old age, which are definitely separate. I belonged more to her youth (there are 17 years between the oldest and youngest child). I gave her this youth and gave her these images: oranges for Christmas, fish on Friday. The fabrics were chosen specifically with my mother in mind. When you get older, you get paler. Sometimes you become invisible, the children don't want to see you, you cannot do as much, and for a lot of old people it becomes a very grey existence. So there is a little bit of colour in there, but she's fading and she's also dropping off the quilt. This is partly because she is not so involved in my life as when I was a child, and partly because several of her children have written her off totally, not accepting her for who she is and not willing to make allowances.

I could not do a painting using such images, because the process does not lend itself to that meditative state that you have when you are working through a very slow process. By the time you have appliquéd one cloud, you have given yourself that concentrated time to go very deep into what you are really trying to do. It allows you time to think.

I made "Free Flight" for my son's wedding. What did I want to say to the couple? I wanted to tell them, "I think it's wonderful." I wanted to give them a larger view of life. So it had to be sky again. I spent a couple of days just painting and painting. I tried to think of being in aeroplanes, with vortexes and wind and everything. I integrated two pieces of fabric so that the line wasn't hard. I wanted it to be a horizon line, but not definite. I did a little more paint spraying and appliquéd more clouds. I needed more colour, so I picked up a basket full of hexagons and threw them on top of the quilt. I realized that was what I wanted: hexagons swirling around. I needed to make some smaller ones, some larger ones. Then it was that laborious appliquéing again! Appliqué has to be done by hand. It has to be invisible – the technique can't intrude.

I started to hand quilt it, but realized that the hand-quilting line was not going to be bold enough, so I started machine quilting these very dramatic lines. It got to be very exciting. You can wreck it when you start machining, because those holes are there. It then needed to be softened up, so I started hand quilting again. It is quite a mixture. Then there came a point when I hated it. I thought it was a vile thing. How could I do that? It was so cute with all those clouds! I finished the quilt and went to Chicago.

When I returned I took my quilts to the exhibition and laid them on the floor. That is when I fell in love with that quilt. I couldn't have been more excited. I realized that there's a continuous train of thought within a quilt, even though it may not be obvious when I'm making it. I trust how I feel, and when I don't, that's when I fail. Whenever I go with the intellectual part of me, I mess it up.

Machine quilting is exciting. It's like being a tightrope walker. You could fall, but you can also get to the other side. If there is no risk, then the work falls flat for me. I

Left: "Sky Flowers", 7' × 6'4" (2.13 × 1.93m), 1986. The reverse of the quilt is shown below left, and a preliminary sketch directly below.

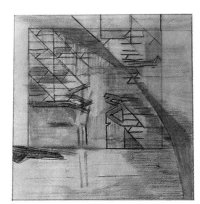

know that if ever quilting stops being exciting and I take no more chances, then it will all be over.

With "Sky Flowers" I was thinking how wonderful the light sky is and chose all my painted, dyed and purchased fabrics that fitted my impression of the moment. We have particularly spectacular skies in California, where weather changes rapidly, and this set the tone of the quilt. Streaks of red became lightning rods, and because I needed to continue my train of thought I finished up on the back (this happens often). The recurring triangles must be birds. I love the way they fly around. Appliquéing has become a meditation time for me, it is so slow – but what a

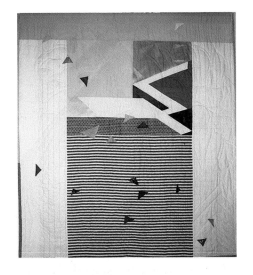

marvellous rhythm!

"Remnants of Deck Chair" is a combination of memories of the Northern Territory in Australia and of London. I remembered a

Right: "Remnants of Deck
Chair", 5'6" – 7'6" × 6'3½"
(1.67 – 2.29 × 1.92m), 1986.

scene in Hyde Park where every-one was out in deck chairs. I took off on a flight of fancy with wind and pieces of deck chair flying around. It truly is an international quilt!

The design for "No Sky in Man-hattan" came as a result of a trip to New York one February to meet my oldest daughter. We had a wonderful time walking all over town, slipping on ice and tripping on the irregular sidewalks in the Village, where we stayed. The sun never came out except for a brief moment while we were walking on Park Avenue. I was looking up and a tall building was suddenly illuminated causing a bronze

shimmer. It was so exciting I stop-ped pedestrians with my outburst and panic to get my camera in position.

The flower shapes came from a visit to Trump Tower after walk-ing too far and being too cold. Entering this luxurious, warm building with its breathtaking riot of flowers perked me up and left me with the two strong visual images of that trip.

It is remarkable to meet third- or fifth-generation quiltmakers. It is wonderful to hear stories of their grandmothers and mothers. I don't envy them, because I am not sure I could deal with that. I am a "quiet radical", in that if there are

Left: ''No Sky in Manhattan'',
7'6'' × 6'7'' (2.29 × 2.01m),
1986. The drawing below
shows how early ideas were
developed. The photograph at
the bottom demonstrates
some of Joan Schulze's
methods for working on a
quilt as large as this.

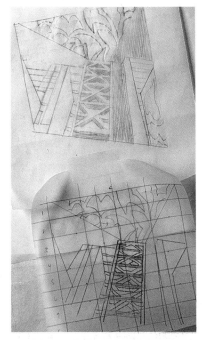

rules, I break them. So I think I would have had a real struggle if my quilting had been inherited. But I like being connected with the tradition. I respect the craft of quiltmaking. That is why I have refined my technique so that I am really good at it. My work always hangs straight. I am not so tied up with the ''appropriateness'' – so many stitches per inch, for instance. You will always find those who are going to say, ''That's not a proper quilt. I've never seen anything like that before.'' When they say, ''Look at her stitches'', they are focusing on the craft.

I like knowing that my quilt could be used on a bed to keep somebody warm. That feels good. It can warm you not only internally, but externally. I still think of how Derk reacted to his quilt. I know that if I were a painter, my kids would not have felt the same way. You cannot wrap a painting around yourself and keep yourself warm with it. A painting is very expressive, it has content, but it doesn't have that sixth dimension, the spiritual and physical warmth. The fact that a quilt is created by your fingers and your eyes, and the feel of it against your skin – that's what makes quiltmaking so exciting!

JUDI WARREN, Ohio, USA

"Santa Fe: Sky Ceremony" was inspired by a visit to Santa Fe, New Mexico. I was overwhelmed by the deep blue-violet of the sky and the unity between the architecture and the land. The fabrics are all hand-dyed, stencilled and painted with textile pigment. It's the first in a series of quilts that deal with specific places that move me or that I love.

"Summerharp" (overleaf) is about my grandfather's sweetpea garden. It grew so prolifically that he had to tie the sweetpeas to his neighbour's garage with green wires; these looked like harp strings.

Below: "Santa Fe: Sky Ceremony", 37" × 48" (94 × 122cm), 1984. A detail of the quilt is shown on the right.

Above: "Summerharp", 5'9" × 4'6" (1.75 × 1.37m), 1985. Hand-dyed cotton has been machine pieced, and decorative areas are hand painted. The quilting is also by hand.

JAN MYERS, Minnesota, USA

I use dyed, pieced fabric. It frees me to work on almost any scale and also involves a sensuous hands-on medium. I am fascinated with colour and light. I play with space and change distances, as gradations of colour move in and out of the pieced surface. I aim to give each work its own light.

Above: "Zion", 30" × 48" (76 × 122cm), 1985. Graduating tones give a strong impression of light playing across the surface of this quilt.

Below: "Red Crazy", 42″ × 55″ (107 × 140cm), 1987. The traditional technique of "crazy" piecing is here used in a modern idiom. It seems that the hundreds of different colours and shapes are about to burst through the restraints of the red and blue lattice work. The detail on the left shows the intricacy of the design.

LINDA KOOLHAAS, Amsterdam, Holland

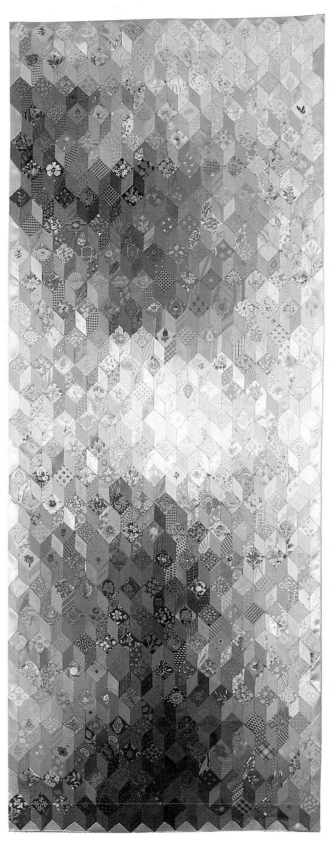

I started about 25 years ago making a rather large tablecloth in hexagons, and progressed to cushions and quilts. These proved to be very good exercises in making well-balanced colour patterns.

I begin with a geometrical design in pencil, so that I have an exact pattern hanging on the wall, upon which I pin the pieces of material, mostly very small. When the colour effect is satisfying, I sew it either by hand or machine. I can't say that I start with an exact idea in mind; the patchwork makes itself.

Left: Untitled quilt, 1984. Regular geometric shapes give a surprisingly soft impression here, achieved with the gentle washes of colour.

Above: Untitled quilt made from pieced strips of irregular length.

DEIRDRE AMSDEN, London, England

Trained as an illustrator, Deirdre Amsden now makes quilts and teaches. She was instrumental in setting up The Quilters' Guild in the UK and continues to be involved in the organization. She has travelled to Soweto, South Africa, and worked closely with the Zamani Soweto Sisters' Council in forming their own quilt group, teaching techniques and producing their own newsletter. Her studio is in London, but she lives in Cambridge.

My mother was always sewing, but I don't think she taught me. She didn't say, "This is how to thread a needle." Nor did she encourage me. I just saw her doing it. She made all our clothes when we were children. I used to go to school dressed in the most extraordinary clothes that I hated.

My mother made patchwork quilts, hexagon ones, all the time. There were always patchwork quilts around, but I didn't really take much notice of them because I didn't particularly like them. I think the reason was because they were simply bits of material sewn together. None of them were quilted, so when they were washed they were all lumpy. They never lasted very long. (I would be interested in them now, though!)

As a child I always made things. I made dolls' clothes and, when older, my own clothes. I was very keen. But I never made patchwork. I wasn't interested in fabric at art school, except for making nearly everything I wore, because as an art student in those days we wanted to put on strange things ahead of time, like the sack dress. I studied illustration at art school. I hated paint, I couldn't sculpt, and I wasn't particularly good at drawing either. So as an illustrator I had to find solutions other than drawing, such as collage, model-making and so on.

I became interested in quilting after I saw an American quilt exhibition in Paris. I thought those quilts were amazing. I had never seen anything like them before. I was familiar with abstract paintings, but never really took to them. Painting doesn't mean that much to me. Those quilts were like abstract paintings in their design, but, being needlework, I could say "I can see how that was done."

Then I went on an embroidery course at the Victoria and Albert Museum and discovered quilting and started to read books. I realized that patchwork wasn't just hexagons. I started to keep notebooks and make patchwork and quilting samples. In every book I read, I discovered something else and would add it to my notes. One day my husband said, "You're never actually going to make a quilt; you're just going to take notes." So I said to myself "I'll show him!"

My first quilt was for a raffle to raise money for an area of Cambridge called "The Kite", because it was going to be demolished. People donated squares of fabric for this quilt. Once you've made your first quilt it's not quite so daunting after that. I then made quite a lot of quilts, mostly fairly traditional, culminating in an exhibition at the library in Cambridge which generated a lot of interest.

I was now determined to quilt

rather than be an illustrator. It was such a liberation to be able to do something I enjoyed at last. It's the fabric. I've always loved materials. When we went to live in America, I mainly took fabric with me. Looking back, I realize this was a strange thing to do, to pack my trunks full of fabric, rather than more necessary things!

My quilts start with a piece of fabric or a group of fabrics. With quilts, unlike painting, you are not faced with a blank canvas. To me that white canvas would be terrible, as would having to mix all my own colours. With quilting, you just have to pick the colours out.

I was presented with this wonderful box of Liberty lawn cottons. I began wondering how I could use them in a blending way, rather than a contrasting way. At art school I remember trying to get watercolour to run across the paper so it merged. You can change the colours, but you have to do it quickly. I wanted to get this smooth wash with fabrics. Pursuing these ideas developed into the "Colourwash" series of quilts. The first quilt was shaded from light at the top to dark at the bottom. I always thought each one would turn out the same, but they never did. I don't know why not. It's a mystery to me! I found the arrangement of fabrics getting light in the middle and dark round the outside, or sometimes quite the opposite!

In one series I wanted the light in the middle: I thought of a spot of sunlight in a forest, or on a floor. (I use a reducing glass and I can instantly see a patch that isn't working.) Later I explored the possibilities of tonal contrasts and this, in turn, led to several larger quilts using a greater variety of fabrics.

There is a contrast all the time

between the quilting and the patchwork. You can get so bogged down at the first stage when you are creating the design, trying to make the fabrics and shapes work together, and you cannot leave them alone. The second stage, cutting all the pieces out and sewing them together, is repetitious. The last stage consists in attempting to make the quilting fit in with the patchwork. I do all my quilting by hand, which is monotonous, but I do like it. Quilting

Below: Early sketches for the "Colourwash" series.

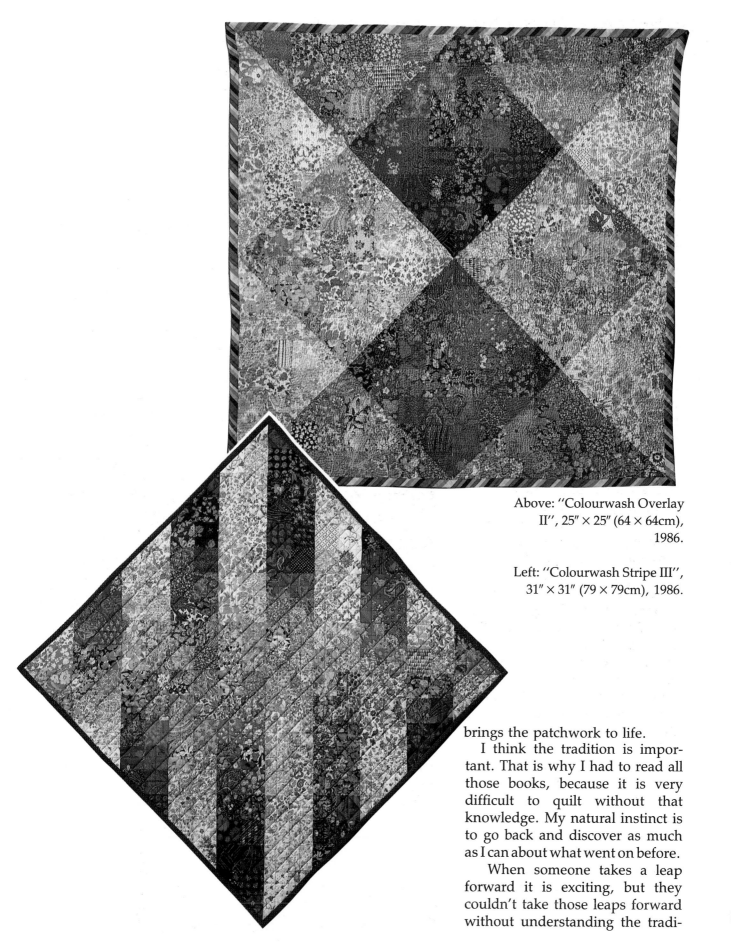

Above: "Colourwash Overlay
II", 25" × 25" (64 × 64cm),
1986.

Left: "Colourwash Stripe III",
31" × 31" (79 × 79cm), 1986.

brings the patchwork to life.

I think the tradition is important. That is why I had to read all those books, because it is very difficult to quilt without that knowledge. My natural instinct is to go back and discover as much as I can about what went on before.

When someone takes a leap forward it is exciting, but they couldn't take those leaps forward without understanding the tradi-

Left: "Colourwash Cubes",
6' × 5'9" (1.8 × 1.75m), 1987.

Below: "Colourwash Stripe
II", 6'2" × 4'5" (1.88 × 1.35m),
1987.

tion. I don't know any quiltmakers who haven't started by making a traditional type of quilt. The idea that you are either an artist or a craftsperson can be restricting and is irrelevant. In America there seems to be a freer use of the terms "art" and "craft".

I sometimes take commissions, as I have to try to earn a certain amount of money. You cannot live in an ivory tower doing just what you want to do. The trouble with commissions very often is that instead of going one step ahead you are marking time or even going back. It is very rare that someone says, "I like your work, so do what you want." It doesn't worry me when I part with my work; it is the making of it that interests me. I hope whoever buys it likes it enough to look after it and use it, but it might be a dog blanket by now! How does one know?

NANCY HALPERN, Massachusetts, USA

Before I made quilts I was an architecture student, and before that a painter. All those influences and former loves combine in my quilts. They are neatly and geometrically constructed out of salvaged, intimate, personal fabric. They are portable shelter. They appeal on a visual level by day, a tactile level by night, and a sensual level at all times. They touch. They wrap. They encircle.

I begin a quilt with an image, an idea, a set of colours, a piece of fabric, or a doodle on graph paper. As soon as the idea takes, I plunge headlong into fabric, like an otter sliding down a bank. As a scrap quilter, I revel in disorderly pools of fabric, where unexpected juxtapositions of colour and texture flash past and can be snagged out. The analogy to water seems to make sense. I have always had barely controlled urges to throw myself into whirlpools and waterfalls, and I delight in submerging myself in fabric.

The end result is much more controlled, but I do aim for a feeling of spontaneity and flow and quickness. I think there are important tensions: immediacy versus elegant technique, pictorialism versus abstraction, fine art versus functional craft. I try to retain these and make them work for rather than against me.

Below: "Floating World II: (Flight of the Gypsy Moths)", 34" × 45" (86cm × 114cm), 1981. This work is machine pieced, but hand quilted.

Above: "Archipelago", 6' × 8' (1.8m × 2.4m), 1983. The symmetry of the houses and trees shows the influence of Nancy Halpern's architectural training. By contrast, the flowing lines of the quilting add life and movement to the work and give increased interest to the subtle play of light and shade. As with "Floating World II", the images give the impression that they are overflowing their boundaries and cannot be rigidly contained within their frames – another way of breaking up the symmetry of the strongest shapes.

MARY FOGG,
Surrey, England

I like to experiment with the expressive effects that can be produced with colour and with combinations of different materials. For example, with "Pigeon" (overleaf) the colours were chosen after the study of a pigeon's iridescent breast. My approach to the

design of a quilt is through the possibilities of fabric, rather than through traditional quilt patterns or modern graphic design. A patchwork to me does not have to be rectangular nor, necessarily, hang flat on the wall.

Below: ''Starlight'', 7'6" × 6'8" (2.29 × 2.03m), c.1984.

Top: "Lantern", 5'5" × 3'8"
(1.65 × 1.12m), 1985.

Left: "Pigeon", 5' × 5'
(1.52 × 1.52m), 1984.

BRIGITTE FISS,
Schülp, West Germany

The idea of "Winter Dream of Summer Garden" came spontaneously while I was skiing in high mountains devoid of colour and warmth. I had a great desire for the flowers and colours of my summer garden, and imagined subdued colours surrounded by coldness. I tried to express this mood in my patchwork. I decided to work by hand. I have not quilted within the patchwork, in order to let the different coloured silks and the lively structures of the material be effective by themselves. Only the border is quilted.

The four little pieces are part of a series of experiments with the impressions of colours, in this case symbolizing the four seasons. I entitled them "Spring", "Summer", "Autumn", "Winter". They're made from painted silk which I cut into pieces. The edges, borders, corners and fringes interest me in particular. They are stitched together to form patchwork. (See next page for illustrations.)

Below: "Winter Dream of Summer Garden", 33" × 33" (84 × 84cm), 1984.

Above: "Spring" from "Four Seasons", 24″ × 24″
(62 × 62cm), 1986.

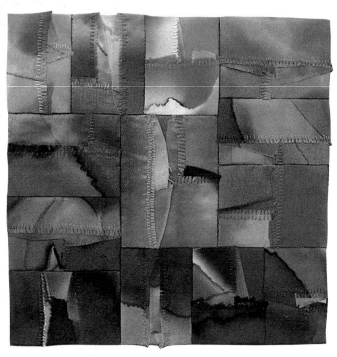

Above: "Summer" from "Four Seasons", 24″ × 24″
(62 × 62cm), 1986.

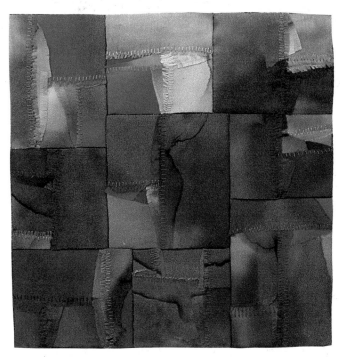

Above: "Autumn" from "Four Seasons", 24″ × 24″
(62 × 62cm), 1986.

Above: "Winter" from "Four Seasons", 24″ × 24″
(62 × 62cm), 1986.

PAM DEMPSTER, London, England

I begin a piece of work by deciding what colours I want to use together. It is important to work out a suitable design that uses the colours to their maximum impact. I never draw up a quilt. I just get out the scissors, rulers and Biro and cut up the material, building the pattern up on a sheet laid out on the floor.

Each quilt I make represents a stage of technical development. Experi-menting with seminole techniques was a particular landmark because they avoid the use of templates and, for me, are a method for building up a quilt top in a free style.

I feel slightly bereft when I have finished a quilt and immediately start on the next one.

Right: ''41-A'', 42″ × 29″ (106 × 74cm), 1987. The juxtaposition of geometric shapes with contrasting colours provides vitality and impact in this quilt. Seminole piecing is a valuable technique for such work.

Above: "Windsail", 45″ × 64″ (114 × 163cm), 1982. This is an imaginative design inspired by a nautical theme. Even though the main shapes of the coloured areas are rectangular or square, the triangular shapes of sails are cleverly implied by the diagonal quilting lines. The motion of the wind is also portrayed by the quilting lines, but in swirls. By reducing her subject to its simplest elements, Pam Dempster has produced an abstract work of art that is both memorable and arresting.

SABINE DU TERTRE, Normandy, France

Sabine du Tertre lives in Varengeville and works at Les Moutiers, an estate which includes a house built by the English architect Sir Edwin Lutyens. Her quilts are experiments in colour, strongly influenced by her surroundings. She has exhibited in France and runs workshops based on her use of colour.

I am interested at the moment in the question, "Why patchwork and not painting?" I find that there is something more in patchwork. I like painting and have been absorbed by it since my childhood, but the problem with painting for me is that I am completely overwhelmed by its history. My approach to patchwork is that of a painter. Materials, with their colours, have their own language which I receive and understand more quickly than that of tubes of paint.

What I like about patchwork is that it gives us something to appreciate as a "whole". There is its tactile quality, its atmosphere, and there is a softness, something that touches us. Perhaps this is because we, as women, are always with fabric – children's clothes, washing, ironing. Why not use it to express ourselves?

I am looking for sensitivity in patchwork, not just technical effect. Technique is only there to help express something. It does not make you any more creative. For me, the whole point is to be completely free with colours, to give the colours room, to work with the composition. Yet it has to be effective as patchwork – so the question "Why didn't I paint it?" never arises.

I believe that up to now materials have not been used in all the ways they could be. Thanks to the diversity in colour, graphics and texture, different materials can create light and dark, movement and perspective and opacity and transparency.

I have discovered that, in addition to sight, I have another sense which helps me with patchwork – taste. When I was pregnant with my first daughter, I had to stay in bed. I couldn't do very much, but I wanted to make something for her birth. So I embroidered. I started to design with colours and suddenly discovered that if I put certain colours together, I felt physically sick! Taste, for me, is inside – in my head and in my body. The colour combinations depend completely on my "taste". Therefore, in order to anticipate effects better, all the senses have to be used which, in my own work, means: taste (colours building), feeling (selection of materials), smell (colours and graphics), hearing (composition and graphics) and sight synthesizing the other four senses.

Inside myself, I have had a dream of beauty, since I was very young, that I am running after – a dream with no design, just pure colour. When I make a quilt I am satisfying that image. It is my way of making the dream a little more concrete. This is why I use patchwork, because with material I can reach my dream quicker.

For me the dream is only intellectual. It provides a framework. I start with an idea, a philosophical idea. I want to ask questions with my patchwork, although I do not

Left: "Brouillard", 4'9" × 3'11" (1.45 × 1.19m), 1983.

always expect to find answers.

I find a structure, a design, which is a symbol of what I am thinking. For example, with "Le Mur" I used a brick (variation on "Tumbling Blocks"). The quilt is about the *non reconnaissance de l'autre*, about the building of walls between people, not wanting to let in the "other".

Using traditional patterns such as "Log Cabin" or "Tumbling Blocks" makes me very, very free. I have used a lot of "Log Cabin" and have stayed with this to be absolutely sure that the effects I produced were the result of my use of colour and composition,

and not because of different techniques and designs.

With "Brouillard" in February 1982 I wanted to make something with no colour. And where do you find no colour? It is in the mist. I was living in London at the time. It is marvellous in England because the outside is very grey, but the cars, gardens, doors and windows are very colourful. So I used what I was seeing around me for making this quilt. Because I was in a town, everything consisted of verticals and horizontals, and I exaggerated these and used "Log Cabin" to represent the structure. With this quilt I used silk and

Above: ''Terre de feu'',
5'8" × 5'8" (1.73 × 1.73m),
1983.

cotton; and the opposition of cotton, thick cotton, to silk gives the same impression of seeing things in a fog. You have flashing colour only.

Then I made ''Terre de feu'' in April of the same year. It was during the Falklands War and the image that came to me combined the iciness of the climate with the fire of the war. In this piece I used silks and velvets. It is divided into two pieces. The bottom is a reflec-

tion of the top, but through water. I had no problem with the technique. It was a game for me. I was interested in the colour, the reflection and playing with the composition. The reflection is not exactly the same because water distorts. People have said to me that you can't see it is a reflection and that I should have done it perfectly. But I didn't want to portray this too clearly, because things never are completely clear!

In painting, when you really want to make something cold you put a little of the opposite, orange for example, and if you want to make something warm you add a little bit of cold. It is a general rule. So to express ice, I put in fire, to make my patchwork more icy.

While I was still living in London I made "Varengeville", which is my home on the Normandy coast. I thought, I am going to imagine "What is France?" from over here, so I made it very, very simple. But I put everything in. There is the

Above: "Varengeville", 5' × 5' (1.50 × 1.50m), 1983.

Above: "Le Mur", 5'6" × 8' (1.65 × 2.44m), 1984.

Above: A quiet place to experiment with colour and texture.

cliff, the mud on the cliff, the stones on the beach. The sun is really pale and you are not really sure it is the sun! I chose the shape and a very simple structure on purpose, to show that structure for me is not important. It is just symbolic. It then allows me to work with the colours. It suits this composition because everything is parallel in that part of the country.

The subject of "Le Mur" is a garden and a wall, and I wanted to make the wall as it is in Normandy, a mixture between grey stones, which come from the sea, and bricks and wood. For this I used lots of different materials. Also for me it was an experiment because I used the basic pattern of the brick. The size of the quilt is exactly in proportion to one brick. I wanted to try and achieve perspective, a sense of space, through both colour and design.

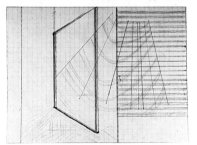

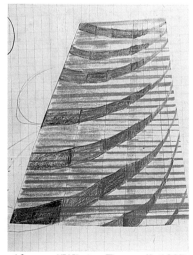

With "Winter Dream" I wanted to get completely away from traditional designs. I had this very strong dream, so I thought it would be very interesting to see what I could do with it. It is about many things, in particular the fading away of a beloved being. I wanted to build the image using a window. The window represents the separation between reality and the dream. I wanted to have a contrast between light and darkness (white and black). I had never used black before. In fact what I wanted to express was: time passing and rising hope (movement and light).

I started by putting together my "palette", collecting all the materials that I would use. I sewed two or three metres of patchwork, building big pieces of colour from very dark to very light. I used strip piecing for this, the best method because it gave me freedom. Afterwards I could cut and change it. I then pinned these pieces on to large pieces of wood in the workshop. While I was making these pieces I didn't cut them at all. It was just like painting. I mixed many different materials and by doing this I made, for example, blackness. If I was painting I would have used some very dark blue: black by itself in painting is dead.

"Rafale" is a quilt made out of woollen materials mostly coming from Ireland. It's a bedspread or wall hanging. It contains my impression of Ireland's atmosphere. *Rafale* in French is a very strong wind that blows from time to time in sudden gusts or blasts. I made this quilt quickly in a very spontaneous way.

Above: "Winter Dream", 1985.

Left: Space for storage of fabrics is essential to any quilter.

Above: "Rafale", 8'3" × 6'7" (2.50 × 2m), 1986.

We are lucky to be working with fabrics. Because of the texture, material has a way of taking light in a very different way from paint. I often imagine myself painting, of progressing with my brush from dark to light, so I try to find that with material. When I draw out my patchwork I never put in the actual colours. I want complete freedom with material, because material is my paint. I think if I had to paint, I would find that medium less rich in nuances.

When I finished "Winter Dream", I didn't want to see it at all. I felt very sad. I didn't want to show it; it didn't feel like mine any more. Technically, it was exactly what I wanted, but I had imagined it to be more intense than that: I find it flat compared with the idea I had originally.

At a certain moment during making a quilt (and you never know when you've reached it), you cannot change anything more. One moment before that, all possibilities existed. You expect to make something really beautiful and you are full of hope. And then the next moment you've gone too far. Suddenly you realize that you have missed something, but you don't know when that was, and now you can't go back; you have to complete it. Afterwards, when it is finished, it has not satisfied the dream.

VIRGINIA RANDLES,
Ohio, USA

I design my quilts with an idea of some sort of pattern. I make rough sketches and lay out a palette of colour in the fabrics I will use. I cut the fabric into general shapes and try these out by pinning them on the wall board in my studio. I prefer using cotton blends, broadcloth or similar fabrics for their sheen and resiliency in quilting, and, for contrast, I have used 100 per cent cottons for their dullness.

If the idea is working, I proceed to draw the blocks on graph paper and make templates. I keep the design in mind, but work in the colour intuitively. I feel free to change direction during the process and I work as long as it takes to produce the idea I have visualized.

"Star Performer" was designed

with chevron-pieced "Log Cabin" pattern using 100 per cent polished cottons and poly batt. It was machine sewn and pressed. It is a transitional piece from star to spiral design.

For "Nebula I" I chose values of greys for the interstellar space with a spectrum of colour for the reflected light. It is strip pieced, machine sewn and machine quilted in cottons and blends with poly batt.

Above and below: "Star Performer", 44" (112cm) in diameter, 1982.

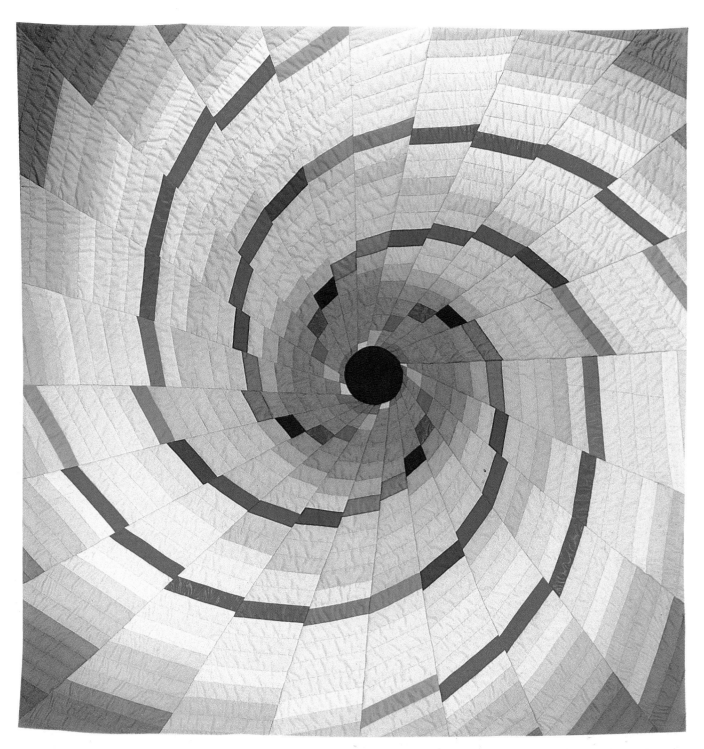

Above: "Nebula I", 52″ × 52″
(132 × 132cm), 1984. Skilful
strip piecing, carefully angled,
provides the basis of the
spiralling effect here. The
brilliant reds, which radiate
from the centre, seem to give
the surrounding pale greys an
almost luminous quality and a
feeling of distance and light.

SUSAN BARTELS,
Karlsruhe, West Germany

I'm a fabric painter. I paint free-flowing or geometric forms, using fibre-reactive dyes on 100 per cent cotton or linen. Sometimes I hang my work free with no backing, other times it is stretched over a frame like an oil painting. Most often I quilt it on molton (a blanket-weight brushed cotton) to give a subtle relief.

I always machine quilt because I like the effect of the continuous line, sometimes accented by thicker thread or contrasting colours. The tight stitch gives the quilting the maximum texture or relief.

I like the double effects of quilts. From afar one sees the painted design and as one comes nearer, the second dimension of the quilt line, the texture, appears.

Right: "Fire", 5'11" × 3'7" (1.80 × 1.10m), 1986. Spontaneity and flowing lines are the main features of this wall-hanging, qualities made possible by the technique of painting directly on to the fabric.

REBECCA SHORE,
Illinois, USA

I start with fabrics (of which I have a large and ever-growing collection) and some idea about what the structure of the quilt will be, although that idea is usually very simple and flexible. For example, I might start by making checked blocks. It is important to remain flexible at all times, because if I predetermine everything the work will become boring and dead. When I start to play with the fabrics within the structure of the quilt, a million arrangements are possible, and I have to choose what I want to show.

Part of making my quilts is

searching for fabrics at thrift stores, and then washing, cutting up and folding them. It is an important time to me, because I can contemplate new possibilities in a relaxed way. During the final process of quilting I look at, think about, and enjoy the piece literally inch by inch. As with the sewing and cutting, it is a chance to experience the piece tactilely. My work is both object and image to me – a three-dimensional thing which I can touch and feel, and a two-dimensional illusion – a world which I can enter into imaginatively.

Right: "Boomerang", 5'6" × 6'1" (1.68 × 1.85m), 1986. Applied fabric scraps show recurring themes of checks and stripes. Their shapes, reminiscent of pattern pieces for clothes, give a personal feel to the quilt.

Right: "Horizon", 44½" × 69¾" (113 × 177cm), 1984. Cotton, silk, rayon, linen and wool are intermingled here. It is the varied assortment of fabric patterns and their arrangement that provide the interest.

RUTH STONELEY, Brisbane, Australia

Ruth Stoneley has been a full-time quilter since 1982. She has exhibited widely in Australia and also in Japan and Indonesia. Her work can be seen in several galleries and many pieces are in various private collections. She has travelled to the United States on a Churchill Fellowship. Ruth teaches and runs a quilt shop in Brisbane and continues to be one of Australia's leading quilters.

I think quilters fall into three categories: those who have always made quilts, putting pieces together to create warm, beautiful covers for their families; those who pursue the craft as a hobby, sometimes following it, sometimes discarding it to try something else; and those who use fabric and thread to express something deep within themselves with the material they know best.

I suppose I started in the first category, making quilts when I had little money but lots of scraps. Now I work quite definitely in the last category, my work tending to end up in galleries, while retaining much of the feeling of creating warm and beautiful pieces.

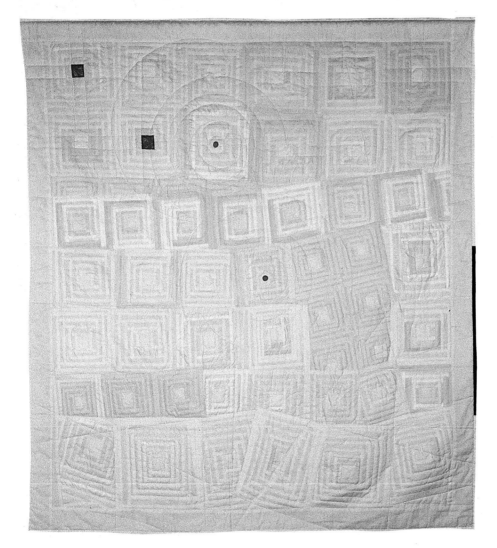

Left: ''Shot to Pieces'', 5'3" × 4'9" (1.60 × 1.45m), 1985. Blood-red splashes add drama to this pale piece consisting of slightly disorderly squares.

Above: "Smashed", 6' × 5'10"
(1.82 × 1.78m), 1983.
Uninhibited use of colour
gives vent to powerful
feelings.

I have a remarkable collection of fabrics. I start with the idea, and the colour, then I select fabrics that fit that idea. I keep a diary, not for every day, but a private sketch book of ideas, thoughts, colours, feelings, rough sketches. I don't do detailed working drawings; the colours and shapes are put together intuitively. I am often asked why I am not a painter. I had no art training, and growing up in a small town in Queensland had very little experience of "art". But I know fabrics. I have always stitched and sewn. I understand the special quality fabric offers.

When I started making quilts I

copied traditional patterns from books. My designs have now changed a great deal, but I have a good grounding in traditional techniques. I machine piece and hand quilt and prefer natural fabrics, cottons and silks particularly, though I sometimes have to use a

synthetic if the colour is right.

I work in a very personal way, expressing feelings and emotions and ideas about myself and others, and the techniques I use are the means of self-expression. If I feel strongly about something, someone, a place or an issue, I can

Above: ''Black Quilt'', 5'4" × 5'1" (1.63 × 1.56m). The quilting lines and the bright streaks of colour relieve the dense background in this purely abstract work.

Right: ''The Favourite Colour'', 6′3″ × 4′11″ (1.90 × 1.50m), 1984. Quite large pieces of silk and cotton predominate in this work, with the quilting lines breaking up their surfaces and forming hexagons, crumpled curves, straight lines, or even hearts. The soft colours evoke a restful mood, demonstrating that Ruth Stoneley is capable of expressing not only powerful emotions but quiet ones, too.

express this in my quilts. For example, ''Smashed'' refers to the feeling of being emotionally smashed.

I made ''Black Quilt'' after an artist friend came and talked, getting to know me before painting a series of portraits. His canvases are big, with lots of dark paint, suggesting to me a black quilt.

I decided to use paint on ''Shot to Pieces''. ''The Favourite Colour'' was created as a bit of a joke on what beds are about!

It is nice to be in a position where quilters are recognized along with engineers, architects and beef producers! Although I am a late starter, having now become established, quilting offers new opportunities and experiences.

YVONNE PORCELLA,
California, USA

I was a handweaver for many years and wove fabrics and accessories. During this time I collected textiles and art books for design sources. I have studied textiles from other countries as well as garments. These serve as design ideas for my quilts.

By using an Olfa cutter my quilts have become more intricate, since I can cut out accurate strips quickly. I like to make quilts with many fabrics, but restrict my piecing to machine-sewn vertical strips. I experiment with painting silk fabric and making silk quilts.

I started to make pieced garments in 1972, which led to quilts. I begin my quilts or kimonos by selecting a colour scheme, and I then decide on the piecing techniques, cutting the fabric and piecing as I go. I do not consider my quilts washable; I prefer them to be wall pieces and not to be used as bedding.

Above: "Sundancer", 4'10" × 5'2" (1.47 × 1.58m), 1984.

Below: "The Odyssey Continues – Resting at Tulare", 6'8" × 3'4" (2.03 × 1.02m), 1987.

ESTHER PARKHURST, California, USA

I consider myself an intuitive self-taught artist and think of my quilts in terms of wall art. For some years I developed my own designs by manipulating and exploring or building with basic elements such as the triangle, square, hexagon, octagon, quarter circle and diamond. I began to develop my own strip-piece methods and soon left tradition behind to claim my own distinct process. My recent work is a strong and personal synthesis of these years of exploration. The process I have developed is tedious and difficult to deal with mechanically, but I love it.

I'm working with movement, the translucent quality of light and shadow, but most of all the properties of colour. These provide a never-ending challenge and sense of discovery. There is constantly a new puzzle to solve.

With "Equatorial Currents" I experimented with a different technique in order to achieve the quality I was after. There is very little strip piecing in it. I literally built this with each narrow strip of fabric. It is machine quilted in the vertical rows and then hand quilted in the coloured areas.

Above: "Equatorial Currents", 5½' × 13' (1.6 × 4m), 1985. Hundreds of tiny fabric pieces have been painstakingly sewn together to create this large wall-hanging. Despite the regularity of their shape, movement is expressed through the sweeps of graduated colour.

URSULA STÜRZINGER, Zürich, Switzerland

My motivation for making quilts does not come from the American tradition. One of my interests is Islamic ornamental design. I make patchwork because I always wanted to do something with my hands!

I am often asked questions about my techniques, such as why I do so much hand work. The questions of "how",

regarding technique, are of secondary importance. More essential for me is "why". I don't consider the time spent on hand stitching as time wasted. It is not an outside discipline which I have to obey; it is one I choose which offers me a structure in which to work towards perfection.

Opposite: ''Output'', 41″ × 37″
(104 × 94cm), 1984.
Traditional techniques and
bold use of colour combine to
make a dazzling design.

Above: ''Kalt-Warm II'',
42″ × 42″ (106 × 106cm), 1986.
A quilt consisting of diagonal
stripes, in which warm
colours offset the cold.

PAULINE BURBIDGE, Nottingham, England

Pauline Burbidge trained at St Martin's School of Art and Design. Her quilts combine technical expertise with striking visual images. She describes herself as a designer/quiltmaker.

I started sewing when I was about ten. I wanted to make a little summer top out of this green and white gingham fabric for myself. I was determined to do it on my own, without my mother's help, because I knew she'd change it. I asked if I could have the fabric, took it up into her bedroom and cut it out under her bed, without a pattern, hoping it would work. But it didn't. It was too small and I couldn't get it on. But I was determined to do things in my own way, without a lot of help. That was my first experience of disappointment in sewing!

At school I was very interested in both painting and sewing. I went to art college, did a foundation course and almost straight away knew I wanted to do fashion design. At that stage, painting, drawing and sewing intermingled. I enjoyed drawing and painting, but knew that if I specialized in fashion I wouldn't do as much of these. So I had to choose to leave the fine art side behind.

I went to the London College of Fashion. It was brilliant for learning technique, but not so good for tuition on design and creative ideas. In the middle of the first year I gathered together a portfolio and took it to St Martin's School of Art and Design. They accepted me in the fashion department. We did fabric printing, weaving, pattern cutting and designing. In the second and third years we were fairly free to get on with our own work and go our own way. For my final show I made a pieced and quilted jacket out of thin strips of coloured satin, tailored to the body. I suppose these were my very first thoughts about patchwork. I hadn't looked at any quilts. If I had done, I would have been really excited, I am sure. But I wasn't pointed in that direction. I thought about fashion, the shapes of the moment and how you can predict them.

I made my first quilt in 1975. I found in a junk shop a book about quilting, *Patchwork Quilts and the Women Who Made Them* by Ruth Finley, published in the 1920s, and bought Ruby McKim's book *101 Patchwork Patterns* as a result. I picked out the butterfly pattern and made it up. I remember I really enjoyed it. Then I started collecting fabrics.

Once I had made one or two small quilts I knew that I wanted to make them full time if I could. I made up a few cushions and similar pieces and took them round the shops. But they took ages to put together and it was impossible to sell them for a realistic price. So I decided that I didn't really want to make cushions and small things, I wanted to concentrate on big pieces, experience making them and develop my own work.

I had to earn some money, so I did freelance dress-pattern cutting for about three days of the week, and spent the rest of the time quiltmaking. I did this for three years and worked towards my first exhibition. This was in Foyle's, and I showed all my work. I made a couple of commissions for friends, although I realized I couldn't live on the kind of money I was charging. If I were to make quilts full time I would have to put my prices up. Having exhibited in Foyle's, I gathered commissions slowly.

I went to the Crafts Council before I had the Foyle's exhibition, to try to get a New Craftsman's grant. I hoped to be able to do less pattern cutting, but I wasn't offered it the first time. I reapplied and was awarded the grant the second time. This meant I could stop about half of the pattern cutting, which really boosted my confidence. In addition to the money, I felt someone was noticing me, and that in itself was rewarding.

My techniques have stayed very much the same throughout the time I have been quiltmaking. I knew that I wanted to use a machine, and I was convinced from the start that I wanted to stick to pieced work because I prefer the limitations of a series of straight lines. I like the graphic image I am able to portray with that, rather than with appliqué. At this time I felt appliqué was so free, I could do anything; it was almost a bit too open. I work closely with traditional American piecing techniques, cutting the fabric out, including the seam allowances, and piecing with the machine. It's the designs that change. I feel that after mastering a certain technique, it is slotted into a box and I'm happy using it. Then my mind is free to think about the design qualities.

Right: "Heron Quilt", 8′ × 7½′ (2.44 × 2.29m), 1981. Strips of fabric are cleverly sewn together to build the pictorial image.

At the very beginning, when I thought of patchwork I just thought of flowery fabric. I bought lots of it, but didn't use any of it in the end! I realized I wanted to work with plain fabrics so that the piecing showed up much more. I'm concerned primarily with the graphic image. But once I've found a fabric that I want to use, I stick to it for a fair length of time. After discarding the flowery fabrics I decided to keep to plain cottons.

I made two quilts in traditional patterns, and then decided that I wanted to work on the theme of pictorial images. I developed the pictorial image in strips, instead of in squares as in the ''postage stamp'' quilts. The ''Heron Quilt'' is a real favourite. I felt that with this I'd accomplished the handling of these strips.

There weren't many pictorial quilts that were pieced, so it felt like a real challenge to make them in that way. I was quite happy working on this theme for a long time, until 1981. It was then that I

Below: ''Eternal Triangle'', 5'6″ × 5'10″ (1.68 × 1.78m), c.1983. An imaginative use of a repeated shape, which also gives a three-dimensional impression.

had the idea of constructing geometric shapes which have an illusion of being three-dimensional. So I made a series of quilts in which I moved away from the pictorial image. "Cubic Log Cabin" and "Eternal Triangle" are both part of this series. These two quilts were designed by simply playing with shapes that I made, using isometric graph paper as a guide. I thought that actual three-dimensional models would be helpful, so I made some out of cardboard, for instance of steps. I used mirrors to reflect these models, thus creating pattern and form to design from. "Liquorice Allsorts" was a quilt from a series that drew inspiration from these models.

"Stripy Step" and "Pyramid in Disguise" both resulted from a drawing which maps out the block shape of the parallelogram. The steps within the parallelogram had great potential for the development of my 3D theme, provided that I handled the tone and colour carefully. I decided to make two quilts from this one idea – one concerned with stripes and one using "crazy" piecing. At this stage I developed the designs further on paper using a full range of colour. The block is repeated in the same way for each. They are constructed entirely by machine piecing and are quilted by machine using silk thread. In "Stripy Step" the idea is that the solid 3D form works totally in the lower right-hand corner, then the shapes are dispersed, gradually

Right: "Pyramid in Disguise", 6′ × 5′6″ (1.83 × 1.68m), *c*.1985. Optical illusion is again exploited to give a three-dimensional effect. The area of "crazy piecing" adds even greater complexity to the design, evident from the detail below.

giving way to plain striped areas. "Pyramid in Disguise" follows a similar theme, but I see the solid 3D shapes emerging from the mass of "crazy" piecing. My eye runs from the top left-hand corner, down to the lower right, as opposed to the emphasis in "Stripy Step".

With many of these 3D geometric ideas, my designs deliberately follow an asymmetrical approach. This is an attempt at making forms less stark, to add freedom within these hard-edged shapes.

At the beginning of my quilt-making I was convinced that I wanted to work with piecing fabric and not appliqué, and I am aware that my new work con-

Above: "Stripy Step", 5'11" × 5'6" (1.80 × 1.68m), 1984. The drawing on the opposite page shows how the design ideas for this quilt were initially worked out on graph paper.

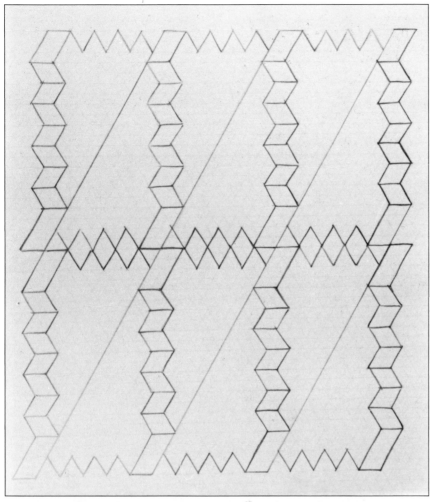

tradicts this. At the same time I believe my recent pieces illustrate the changing and growing aspects of contemporary quiltmaking.

Early in 1986 I made a series of torn-paper collage studies and decided to base my new work around these. I wanted my quilts to "loosen up" and get away from the tight, rigid quality of the geometric pieces. Therefore I have added fabric collage to my techniques, together with free stitching on the fabric surface.

"Lowestoft" is a quilt which has resulted from a work made while on a school residency at the Benjamin Britten High School in Lowestoft. I completed a series of both paper and fabric works, based on the subject of the docks. This quilt design was created from a study of a boat in dry dock being painted.

"Kate's Vase" is a small wall quilt with repeated images that are taken from a still-life set-up. The shapes are identical, but the network of stitching changes dramatically from the top left-hand corner to the lower right corner. This work has been purchased by the Victoria and Albert Museum.

The tradition of quiltmaking has a strong influence on my work. Although I have not stayed within the traditions of the craft visually any more, I'm still sticking quite closely to inherited techniques. Looking at antique or contemporary quilts plays a big part in my enthusiasm for the craft. For instance, I find Amish quilts very exciting with their colour and their simplicity. I see myself continuing in a fairly traditional way, but with new imagery.

There is a history of quiltmaking in the UK as well as in America, but quilts have been so much more important in American history. They have been a part of their families' lives and, because of this, lots of people collect quilts

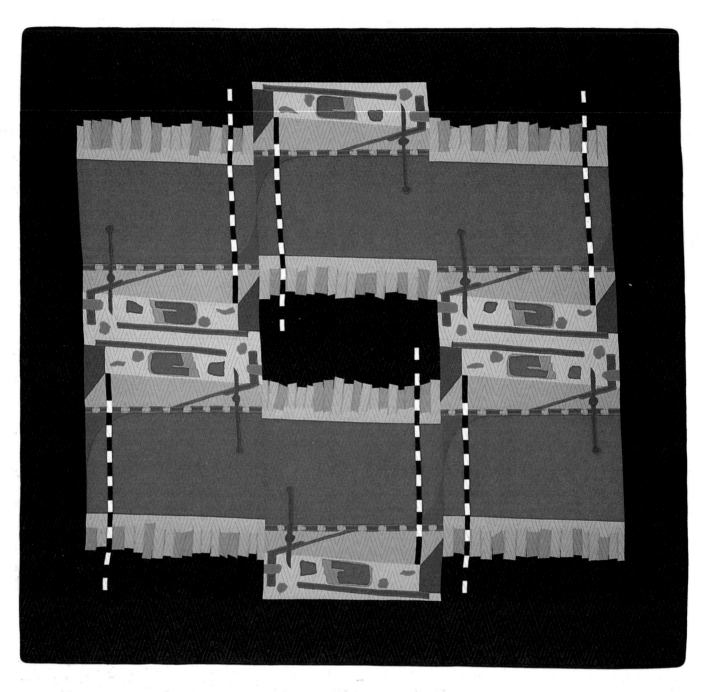

and put them on public display. Their value is fully recognized.

I like to class myself as a designer/quiltmaker. I'm not a fine artist. If I were painting I would be continually involved emotionally. As it is, I enter this state when I am designing a quilt, but am relieved from it while sewing. That's great, because I enjoy both the designing and the time spent making the quilt. I wouldn't want to be a fine artist all the time, because the emotional state of mind would be too much for me.

I still like to make large quilts, the size that will throw over a bed. It is the quilting that makes them really manageable and firm. If the fabric is just pieced and then hung up, it is dull and lifeless.

I started lecturing and taking workshops in 1979. At first I did a very general workshop. They then became much more specialized. Initially it was quite a small part of my income. I do enjoy the teaching, the contact, seeing people, but the main thing is to continue with my own work.

Above: "Lowestoft I", 55" × 58" (140 × 147cm), 1987. Inspired by seeing a boat in dry dock being painted, Pauline Burbidge has taken the barest elements of her theme and created them into a striking image.

Above: Kate's Vase'',
35″ × 35″ (89 × 89cm), c.1987.
The differences in this
repeated image are very
subtle, since they consist
purely of a change in the
network of stitching.

SYLVIA ZUMBACH,
Wetzikon, Switzerland

My quilts are the result of my love of classic simplicity, of my pictorial ideas, and of my joy in mastering manual techniques. My pictorial ideas are complicated and I have tried to fit them into the strict structures of the American pieced quilts.

Below: "Log Cabin: Variation XXI"

Above: "Drei Berge". The
impression of three mountain
peaks emerges primarily
through colour from these
regular pieced triangles.

SONYA LEE BARRINGTON, California, USA

While I am constantly hopping back and forth between dark and light colour choices, symmetrical and asymmetrical settings, the unifying elements in my work are the use of the checkerboard and curvilinear patterns. My work can be categorized as "in series". I prefer to break it down to several "sub-series". I hope that it will be ever-changing and growing, but know deep down that I (probably) will always work with curves and checkerboards. I am interested in making more "shaped" pieces and getting away from the square or rectangular format.

Above: "Shore Break",
30" × 42" (76 × 107cm), 1986.
The movement of waves gave
the impetus to this shaped
work.

Above: "If you drink, don't
drive", 25″ × 25″ (64 × 64cm),
1986.

NELL COGSWELL, Massachusetts, USA

I've been making quilts with a very large abstract overall design and have done away with the block altogether. This entails drafting out the final design on a very large sheet of brown wrapping paper to actual size. This is then cut up, piece by piece, and the pieces used as the actual templates.

The appeal of quilts lies in the fact that you can pick a quilt up, handle it, feel it, fold it, put it over you. It is soft. The surface, with its quilting, has a subtle three-dimensional quality that invites people to touch it. Have you ever watched people at a quilt show? Even with ''Do not touch'' signs in evidence, you see people's hands running gently down the quilts' edges to gauge the thickness, the ''feel'' of the fabric, the stitching. The associations in the mind with quilts are of home, warmth, sleep and love – something lovingly made by hand for someone's comfort.

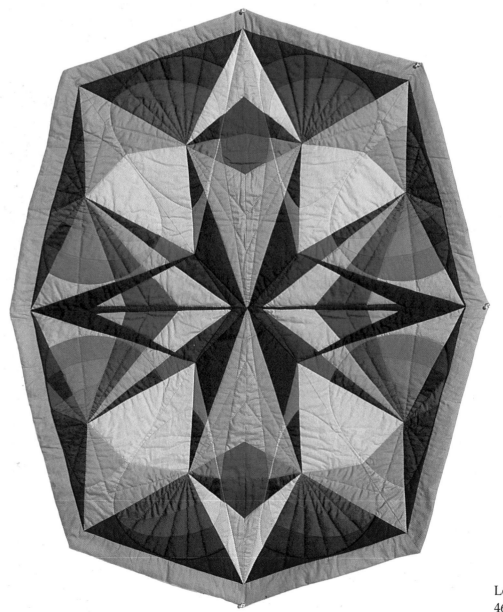

Left: ''Seed Crystal I'',
46" × 38" (117 × 97cm), 1986.

EDITH RAYMOND, Paris, France

I am a quilter, an embroiderer and an illustrator of children's books. In my work as an illustrator I have to meet deadlines, and produce drawings within prescribed briefs. Making quilts gives me the opportunity to work freely, exploring my own feelings and creativity. What interests me mostly in patchwork is graphic design.

Often I start by making a fabric collage. I like strong colours, sometimes using all black or all white. I work a lot on the theme of the labyrinth, which fascinates me because of its graphic "game" and the

symbolism. I am also very interested in letters and numbers.

I use the surface as an extra element which gives another direction to the labyrinth. All the surfaces are quilted by hand, which allows me the time to think about what I am doing, even though the design has already been worked out. I can modify it as I go along and can change it if I'm not satisfied with it. I put together my quilts by machine.

In some patchworks of the labyrinth I have put a mirror, in which people looking at the patchwork see themselves.

Below: "Labyrinthe noir et jeune" – black and yellow labyrinth.

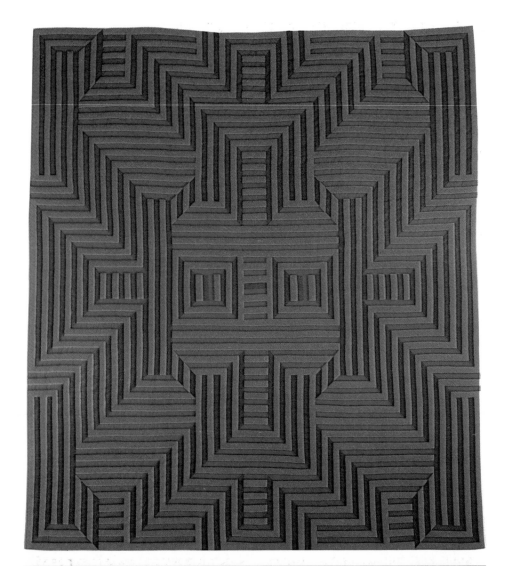

Left: ''Labyrinthe vert, bleu, rouge'', 5′4″ × 4′8″ (1.63 × 1.47m), 1987. The detail underneath shows the complexity of the piecing.

ESTHER BARRETT, Gloucestershire, England

Esther Barrett operates from the Cirencester Workshops. She studied embroidery at art college, during which time she became interested in antique quilts. Her own quilts have developed from the techniques used in traditional quilts, particularly the textures created by the inclusion of paper templates.

Part of what attracts me to patchwork is its repetitiveness. I was originally interested in printed textiles, because of the repeating images. At college embroidery was my specialization. I did my thesis on patchwork. I see patchwork as a part of the "embroidery world", not as a separate entity. As far as I'm concerned, patchwork is an embroidery technique. I went round museums looking at old patchwork, and on lots of them I thought the back was more interesting than the front. They had old newspapers and letters tucked in. They were beautiful textures. I thought I could reverse the process and use the back of a quilt as a front. So I did some samples and this was how I came to do "Stitched Stripes". Traditionally, you take all the papers out of the quilt when you've finished, but I thought it would be interesting to make them part of the design.

I looked at a lot of American quilt books and I found their arrangement of colours quite fantastic. They influenced my own use of colour. Previously I worked with softer colours. My use of fabrics now isn't at all traditional, because I mix together all different kinds of materials, rather than keeping to one particular sort.

I use a lot of stripes (which are machine sewn), a combination of "Log Cabin" and seminole piecing. At other times I use hand techniques, as in the template patchwork where the papers are left in. With this technique, in which the reverse side is exposed, all the stitching remains, including the tacking stitches. I contrast the fabric colours with different col-

Right: A sample book provides a record of ideas and a source of inspiration.

oured threads, so that the stitches add to the overall texture. The papers I leave in are often postage stamps and from maps so that their colours and printed qualities also add to the surface texture.

"Stitched Stripes" is really in the form of a sampler. I think with this particular sort of design it is important that each square is individual, but that they all fit together and create a whole.

The "Plain and Patterned" wall hanging is more traditional. I have used stripy patchwork but have mixed it with plain coloured geometric patchwork. The whole thing was machine pieced. I have also quilted this piece of work, one of the few times I have done this. I was pleased with this quilt because I felt it was a step forward. Mixing the plain with the striped worked well, but it is not an area I really want to pursue. I have become more interested in developing the "reverse side" texture.

I make drawings and samples while I am gathering my ideas. With the "reverse side" patch-

Left: "Stitched Stripes", 1980. Many imaginative arrangements of colours and patterns are to be found here within each square, giving a kaleidoscopic effect.

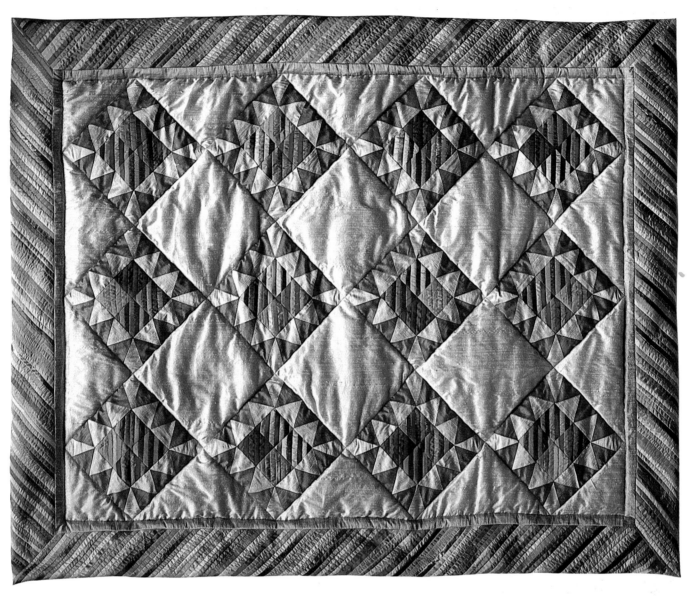

Above: "Plain and Patterned", 4' × 5' (1.22 × 1.52m), 1982.

Right: This shows how Esther Barrett creates interest from "reverse side" patchwork. Postage stamps are used as paper templates.

work, one piece suggests the next. I make lots of samples, then do a rough outline on paper. This gives me more flexibility. It is important to be able to feel my way along with some pieces. I discard very little while making a quilt, but if I come to a piece I don't like I just chop it out and put it somewhere else!

"White Squares" was a commission and was a really enjoyable project. It was a challenge to use only pale colours. "Square Delight" was also a commission. I used lots of patchwork techniques, although I found the size limiting.

"Summer Haze" contains a mixture of different patchwork techniques, but includes a specific idea as well. It was designed as a whole piece, rather than sampler pieces. To start off with, I wanted to do a quilt based on gardening. I like flowers and trees. I did lots of scribbles in my sketch book, made some samples and gradually the idea changed from a garden to a summer day, the smell of grass, the breeze. Before, it was the patchwork techniques that caught my imagination, but with this quilt it was the idea, and I was able to use my techniques to carry out the idea. This is one of the areas I want to spend more time exploring – taking specific ideas and using patchwork to illustrate them. I would like to try making more pictorial wall hangings as well as the patterned and sampler ones.

I feel more confident now. I am

Above: "White Squares", approximately 24" × 36" (61 × 91cm), 1983. Texture becomes particularly important when colours are of a similar tone.

Above: "Square Delight",
approximately 18" × 18"
(46 × 46cm), 1983. The main
skill lay in joining together so
many small pieces.

Right: A "reverse side"
patchwork is created here by
using the seam allowance of
each large white triangle to
form a frame for the small
coloured one. Frayed ends are
part of the work.

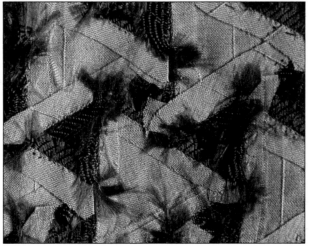

Left: "Summer Haze", approximately 60" × 36" (152 × 91cm), 1983. A traditional quilt in which colour and surface texture evoke shimmering heat.

more proficient on the sewing machine and much more sure of my use of colour. I get varied responses. Many people can't cope with the raw edges and the papers being left in because it's "going to fray" and "you can't wash it". These aspects distress them. I think it's important that the traditional techniques should be kept alive and not lost.

INGE HUEBER, Cologne, West Germany

When I began quilting I only varied the traditional forms a little. Sticking too rigidly to tradition, however, soon began to restrict me. So I began experimenting. I have not found the tradition a burden, more a starting point for my own ideas. Making only traditional quilts dispenses with a wide realm of possibilities. That seems to be the reason why patchwork has hitherto been seen as a craft and not an art.

I use cottons which I dye myself. The colours form the basis of my quilts. When I start a quilt I search from this abundance of colour for a particular palette, either clear leading colours, or various strengths of one colour. I cut up the material, mainly using the seminole technique. The pieces are sewn together, cut, then sewn together again. This doesn't happen according to a set plan, but from ideas as they occur and through experiment. Chance and unpredictability are the characteristics of this technique.

I hand quilt. The quilting is based on the surface design and structure of the material and the technical

Below: "Up and Down", (2 × 2.50m(6'7" × 8'3")), 1984.

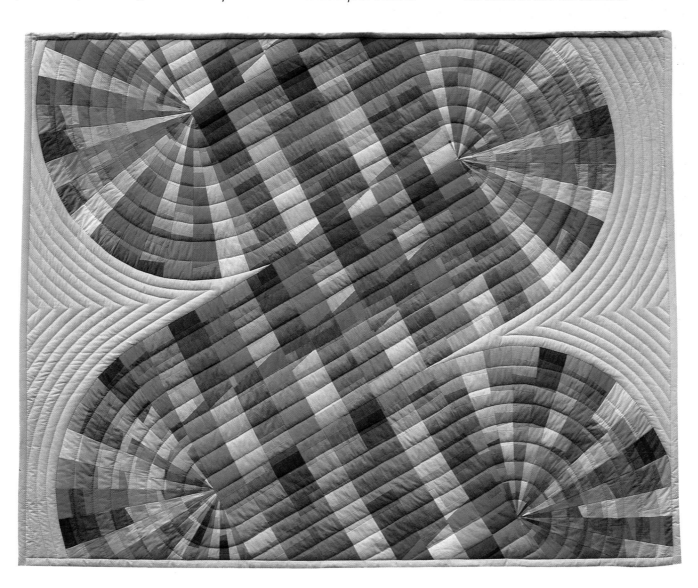

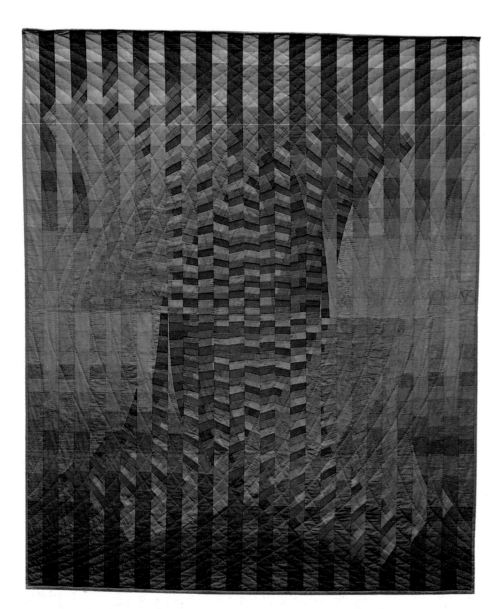

Left: "Reflected Image",
7'10" × 6'6" (2.38 × 1.98m),
1985. Hand-dyed cottons help
to create the extraordinarily
subtle effect in this quilt.

*possibilities of the stitching and
quilting. This on the one hand
presents a restriction in comparison,
say, to painting, which is clearly a
freer medium. On the other hand,
through these limitations the
techniques actually offer possibilities.
The cutting and putting together of
materials allows the spontaneous
association of colours.*

*The quilting alters the smooth
surface, creating light and shadow,
and adding another aspect to the
design. This three-dimensional effect
is only available to painters through
the physical build-up of paint.*

PAMELA GUSTAVSON JOHNSON, Missouri, USA

I am sometimes asked why I make quilts instead of paintings. First, I have always loved making things. Second, fabric can do things that paint simply cannot, and discovering new fabrics has the excitement of working with found objects. For example, ''Black and White Log Cabin'' was made in response to a fabric printed in black and white triangles.

Most of my quilts are systematic variations of traditional quilt patterns. However, I do not believe that the tradition is served by simply repeating it. My intention is to expand on what has gone before in ways which reflect my particular interests, such as colour theory and the aims of non-objective art.

Finally, the soft, warm, emotional qualities of quilts make them remarkably attractive objects. The same geometry executed in paint often has less universal appeal. Hence the quilt medium can be seen as a device to seduce people into looking.

Below: ''Black and White Log Cabin'', 48½ × 48½" (123 × 123cm), 1985. Machine-pieced cotton, hand quilted.

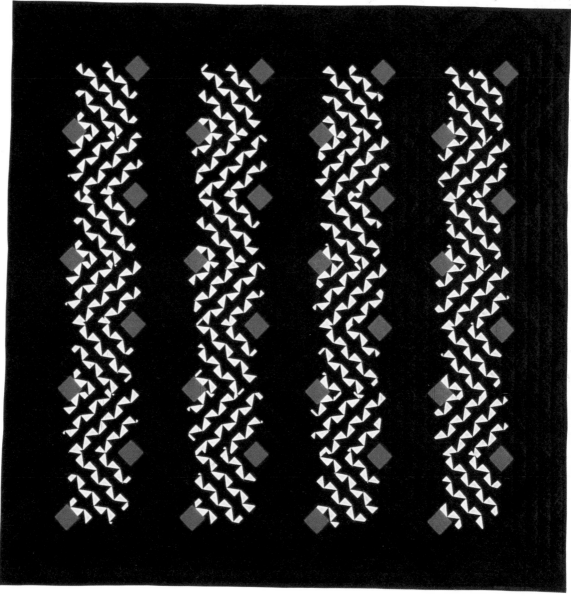

FAYE ANDERSON,
Colorado, USA

My background is in advertising design and I approach my stitching as if I were doing an illustration or a layout for a print ad. Using fabrics instead of paints to develop images brings the added interest of patterns and textures that can be lively and rich.

"Plane Geometry" is part of a series using "New Wave" colours and shapes set against a printed grid work.

In "3 Dog Night" three dogs are cavorting in a snow storm and hailing dog bones, in the centre panel, and their spirits are playing in the borders that show their favourite seasons and past times. "3 Dog Night" is of Eskimo origin, the night temperature being calculated by the number of dogs they needed to sleep with to keep warm . . . three dogs is very cold!

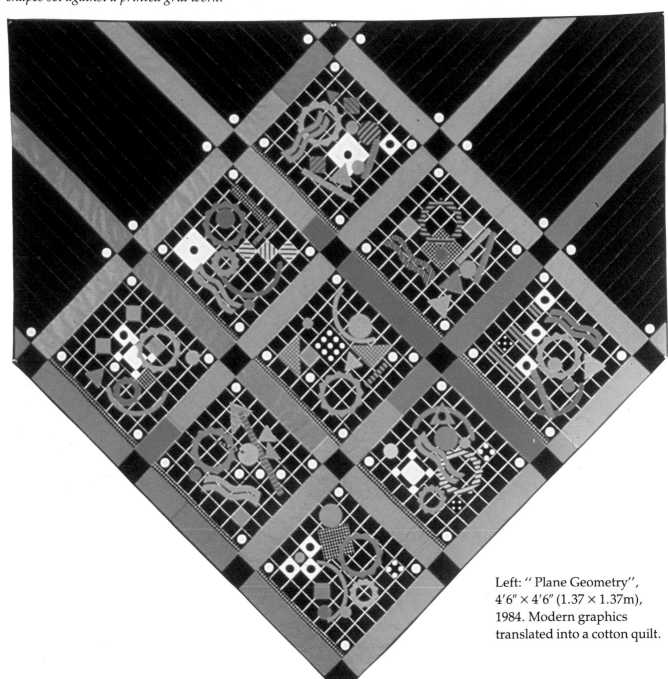

Left: " Plane Geometry",
4′6″ × 4′6″ (1.37 × 1.37m),
1984. Modern graphics
translated into a cotton quilt.

Above: ''3 Dog Night'',
4'5" × 3'10" (1.32 × 1.17m),
1984. Vivid colours and lively
imagery create an unusual
wall-hanging.

JEAN HEWES, Texas, USA

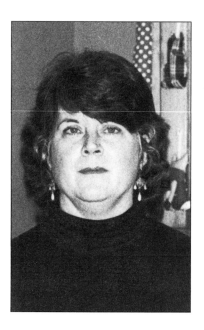

Jean Hewes spent eight years in California's "Silicon Valley" making quilts. She has exhibited widely, including the Quilt Nationals of 1981, '83 and '85, and her work has been reproduced in many publications. She won the Domini McCarthy Award for Exceptional Craftsmanship in 1983, and now lives in Forth Worth.

I started making quilts to escape a trap, the trap of child-raising. American women have traditionally quilted to escape bleak environments. Child-raising for me meant sitting at home with diapers, runny noses and kids fighting. I have an MFA in ceramics, but ceramics meant a great deal of equipment in a large room, a messy medium that didn't combine well with children and their problems. I've always sewn most of my clothes, so I had access to a large quantity of fabric scraps. Quilts can be made in a small space. They are a convenient medium, a release into dazzling colour and intricate patterning.

I don't make sketches to begin quilts. I work with colours, patterns and textures. Shapes suggest themselves and interrelate, and the quilt takes on a life of its own. I start with a basic background cloth, or machine-piece fabrics together to make a background cloth. I pin batting and lightweight fabric behind and into the background cloth and pin the entire piece to the wall. I design the piece while it is on the wall.

I dye large amounts of silk, using Procion dyes and what I call a "slap-dash" approach to batik. I don't use batik to draw figures. I apply wax patterns and colour after colour until I get a piece of fabric that fits my purpose. I cut the dyed silk into pieces and fit the pieces into patterns to make body parts and other shapes.

I also use some fabric yardage other artists have given me, which they have rejected for their purposes, as well as embroidered Indian and Afghan materials. Many of these fabrics I re-dye. I use them like my own dyed silks, cutting out smaller shapes and eventually quilting designs into them.

Often I dye different weights and textures of silk in the same dye baths to achieve colour variations. Recently, I have been layering silk gauzes over other silks to veil harsh colours, creating illusions of depth and translucencies. My interest in veiling goes back to my stay in Iran (where women wear veils) as a Peace Corps volunteer in the late '60s.

I consider my quilts works of art, and believe that each viewer appreciates a work of art according to his or her background. I also see quilting as a story-telling medium. I lived in California and worked on quilts for eight years. The 11 quilts I made there, starting with "The Sitter", are a journey through the flashy society of Silicon Valley, people uprooted, but highly motivated. My quilts show life in the fast lane, a deadly, highly competitive society, clothed in a colourful environment.

In my quilt "The Sitter", I see myself plonked down into plum surroundings with my creative tree ablooming. I had previous ties to the San Francisco Bay area and

Right: "The Sitter", 5'5″ × 4'6″
(1.65 × 1.37m), 1978.

Right: Detail of "The Sitter".
Hand-dyed fabrics are used
for artistic effect.

when my husband's company transferred us there, I thought I knew what life was going to be like. "The Sitter" is securely placed in her chair. However, there is a malignant growth in the background.

In "Streamers", the damsel in distress is mired in lovely chaos, menaced by an uncertain creature who is pushing her back into an abyss. "Flower Girls" shows a baton threatening females. The targeted female is above and apparently unconnected to the surrounding unpleasant faces. The "Wizard" is hiding behind the face mask, hoping his actions can't be correctly interpreted. He wears both angel wings and bones on his back.

Who are these people? Silicon Valley brought in a new parade. It was crowded with technicians, people with very specific jobs and predetermined (narrow!) outlooks. They enjoy the physical life and huge salaries. They pay vast sums of money for property, creating a real estate boom which has rocketed small property owners into the status of the wealthy. My California quilts are a personal, visual diary. To my

Below: "Streamers", 6'1" × 7'2" (1.85 × 2.18m), 1981.

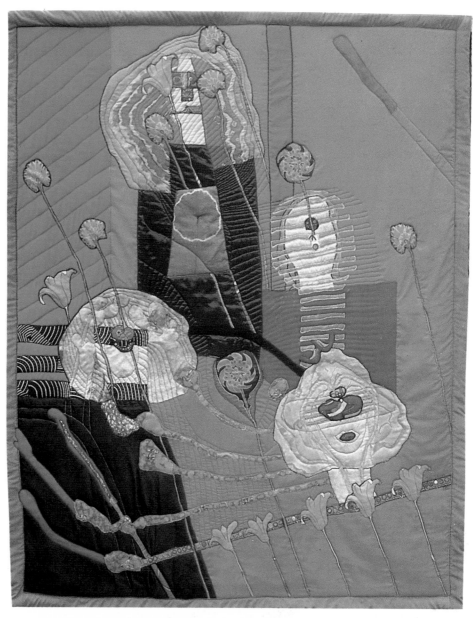

Right: "Flower Girls",
5'8" × 4'7" (1.73 × 1.40m),
1982. Like many other quilts
by Jean Hewes, this one tells a
story. Behind the bright
façade of life lies the grotesque
reality.

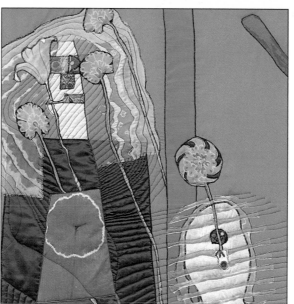

Right: Detail of "Flower
Girls".

Above: "Wizard",
6'11" × 5'11" (2.11 × 1.80m),
1983. Another character from
the Silicon Valley series, who
hopes that his real intentions
cannot be detected.

Above: "Circus", 7'4" × 8'6" (2.24 × 2.59m), 1987. Quilts, for Jean Hewes, provide an opportunity for recording the events of her life in a symbolic way. The creatures in "Circus", although weird, are less grotesque than those in the Silicon Valley series. A note of optimism creeps into her work as she moves on to a new phase in her life.

mind the Grinch (Silicon Valley) ate the beautiful, fragile, mellow California I used to know.

After eight years of life in Silicon Valley, my husband changed jobs and we moved up to the stratosphere, the land above it all, the state of Texas. My quilt "Circus" shows an ambiguous jewelled environment, a space above, peopled with fanciful creatures.

SUE ALLEN HOYT,
Michigan, USA

I love to quilt, and all but one of the quilts I have ever made has been hand quilted. I am also very interested in interlaced patterns, and dense and elaborate surface encrustations of, well, things! I embroider the fronts and sew on glass and metal beads and ornaments (for instance, titanium drops, 14-carat gold and glass beads, mica washers, Egyptian paste).

These quilts are part of a series of fan shapes that I started making, as I was tired of four corners. I chose fans because they have a pleasing, variable shape, lending themselves to asymmetrical treatment.

I wanted to base "All the Colors of Darkness" on the same kind of sliced design, but using the dark colours that I love especially. The idea was to make it a densely encrusted, highly ornamented piece that you have to look and look at in order to see everything that's there. I inlaid one of the striped parts with copper lamé to give it sparkle, like a surprising little meteor-trail lighting up the dark.

"Darkness Visible" uses the same techniques of inlaid patchwork, but has more embellishment. "Eidolon" is two intersecting fans cut by a sort of prism-like pillar.

Above left: "Darkness Visible", 1985. Inlaid patchwork adds sparkle to the deep tones, as shown in the detail on the left.

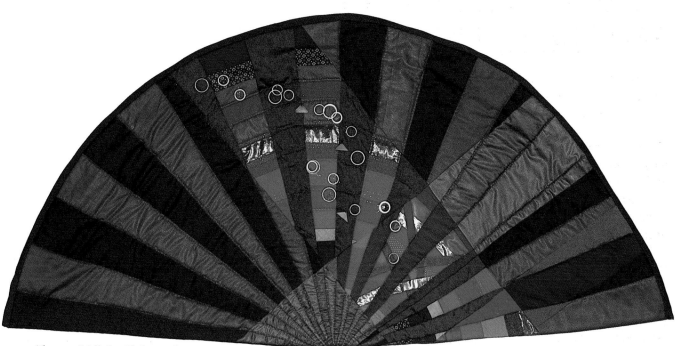

Above: "All the Colors of
Darkness", approximately
22″ × 45″ (56 × 114cm), 1984.

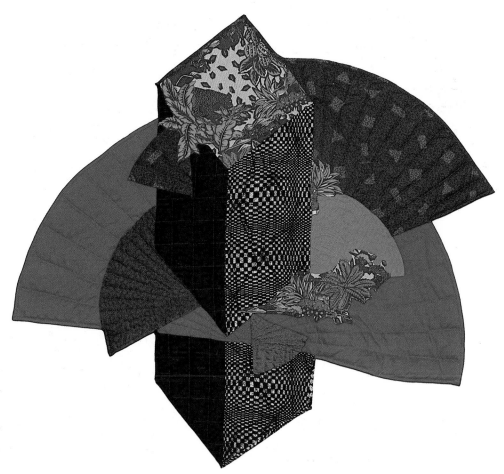

Right: "Eidolon",
approximately 45″ × 45″
(114 × 114cm), 1986. The idea
of the fan shape is further
developed by the introduction
of the contrasting pillar.

BARBARA HARROW,
Southampton, England

I am an artist working with cloth in the same way that a painter works with paint. I respond to the life which I feel in the cloth when I'm creating a quilt and I listen intuitively to the colours. I never draw a design but work directly with the colours, the feel, shapes and movement, and as they grow I build the quilt.

What interests me is the communication with the creative forces which produce my work, and my amazement at their beauty, power and energy.

Working mainly with colour I have developed my ideas of creating "living sculpture" into a performance company of three. The performers' skill is to inject the colours and shapes with life, movement and energy. The result is a unique art form that is intended to stimulate the audience and inspire them to appreciate colour and shape in a new way.

Although my work leans towards sculpture, I maintain a very high level of craftsmanship and use the techniques of quilts to create beautiful sets and costumes for the performances.

Below: "Backdrop". The form and design of this quilt grew spontaneously from the colours themselves.

The two figures on this page are examples of quilt sculpture, an entirely original art form developed by Barbara Harrow.

DINAH PRENTICE, Northampton, England

Dinah Prentice began by making traditional quilts and has in recent years developed her work to include techniques and images from her earlier time as a painter. Her quilts are large and powerful and include many references to her political and philosophical beliefs.

I started by making traditional quilts, which were separate from the collages and paintings I produced. The first one was for my daughter. We were living in the country at the time. It was winter and we were all very cold.

I needed to make some money so I started producing quilts to sell to various shops. The quilts got larger and larger, 6 ft, 7 ft, 8 ft (1.8 to 2.5 metres), as I learned to handle huge spaces. They were tough and brown and structural, yet contained this wonderful softness, a wonderful density, and an enormous amount of work.

I kept looking for different ideas. For example, I made a block using the positive/negative image of Arab tiles of birds, in which both shapes are absolutely identical, but I had the feeling that I was just dredging around for ideas. I thought I would try making a quilt out of my collages, and do in quilting what I had done in my large-scale paintings. There's a quote from Robert Rauschenburg, "What gets an artist out of his chair is a mixture of thoughts", and that's what got me into my studio sticking big pieces of paper together and working out grids. I knew I wanted to sew, and I knew I wanted that soft quality.

My collages had always been to do with edges and to do with lettering. We used to live in a village miles from anywhere and my children were supposed to do the paper round. But the papers seemed to come after they went to school, so mother took the round! The bag was marked COVENTRY EVENING TELEGRAPH, printed in black on white canvas. What pleasure the edges of the lettering gave me!

About the same time I saw an image of a Red Guard in China writing messages on enormous bits of paper that filled half a junction of main roads that went off into the distance, with no towns, no trees, no nothing – just bare. It was surreal. There was this tough-looking Red Guard making marks that don't make any sense to us. The fact that I couldn't understand it didn't matter. I saw this Chinese image and it made me gasp, and it's still tucked away in my mind.

Another image came from a Donatello relief. It's a low relief, about a quarter to half an inch (6–12mm), no more. The crown and the crucifixion are expressed in half an inch of clay. (Donatello produced this exquisite intellectual combination – the drawn line which gives perspective, and the form.) Of course there is no actual drawing in relief; the form is created by the deepness of the shadow. That was years and years before I made anything soft. I realized later that this was what I wanted in quilting. I want that little soft bit of depth and I am getting closer and closer to that quality of cast shadow.

The first quilt which seems to me to bring many of these ideas and images together is "A4". It

Opposite: "A4", 9' × 10' (2.74 × 3.05m), 1981.

was a great emotional effort to make. Outside was the village, the fête, coffee mornings, everybody still thinking I was making my traditional quilts. Inside I was doing something which I didn't understand myself. Subconsciously I was revealing a lot of the things that I thought and felt. So I had found a structure which was able to hold me for the first time. "A4" was a radical change. I was shocked by it because it had everything in it I wanted to say.

"A4" started with a drawing of a page of lettering. I had to make a grid and then enlarge it. I ended up with a full-scale drawing of "A4". I then cut a bit out of it, put it on my table and worked out how to cut the shapes in fabric, because I could only manage a T-junction on the sewing machine! Each time, I sewed the shapes together and put the bit I'd sewn back in place of the drawing.

By this time we had moved to the house I live in now. It's important, because I have much more room here and the children have grown up and gone. A lot of what I do is informed by my painting experience, the knowledge of what painting is and of art history.

Below: "Perspective Drawing", 7'2″ × 8'4″ (2.18 × 2.54m), 1982.

Above: "Molesworth Mon
Amour", 6'11" × 8'2"
(2.11 × 2.49m).

I am fascinated by the aesthetics
and technicalities of making
space. In "Perspective Drawing" I
wanted to make space, so I decided to tip the plane of the drawing, dropping it down to create
perspective – hence the name.
Similar to "A4's" connection with
lettering, "Perspective Drawing"
was originally done from punctua-
tion marks.

For a previous quilt, I had
shaded in the different tones on
the pattern. I wanted to put this
effect on my next quilt. The local
art shop suggested a spirit-based
ink for drawing on silk, so in
"Perspective Drawing" there are

large pieces of silk that I have
drawn on and then cut and used.

Now the story of "Molesworth
Mon Amour": I had a paper bag
from the Tate Gallery and it was
the red lettering on the bag that
attracted me. I cut the lettering up,
arranged it and made a collage.
(At first it was called "The Red
and White Collage".) I then
photocopied it. I started to paint
the photocopies, but as I was
painting, ideas came together. I
had seen a newspaper photograph
of women pinning things to the
fence at Greenham Common.
(Greenham and Molesworth are
both American airbases in Eng-

land where there are women's peace camps.) At first I thought what a mawkish, sentimental thing to do. But obviously it must have become etched into my thinking process and in fact I'm entirely in sympathy with what they're doing. I drew and then painted the grid on to the photocopy, and then of course the grid became a wire mesh.

I found myself painting a dead grey across that. I feel emotionally about this sliding wide grey, this grey which is neither white nor black, which has something to do with people who won't make up their minds whether they are for or against important issues. I started to paint yellow on the background. I painted it down as I would paint a wash on paper. There was this constant dialogue going on in my head between emotion and technique. I was also

thinking of poison sinking down, of death, but I stopped this wash flowing after two inches (5 cm). So now a dull yellow had affected the greys, turning them into an orangey-yellow.

The collage was still an unnamed thing. On one occasion I walked into the room and thought "Molesworth Mon Amour", this poetic copy of the film title. I was shocked! But once I had the name, I made the quilt and into the making I put all the support I felt.

"Catalonia Stomp" was a response to a lyrical holiday driving through Spain for the first time: mountains, wine, nationalism, the Prado and Toledo, Barcelona and Picasso – a heady mix. In contrast, "Doorway" was a reaction to that obscene genocidal war in Lebanon. I saw the broken doorway as a metaphor for the men's guns in the hills destroying the women's

Opposite: "Catalonia Stomp", 6'8" × 5'6" (2.03 × 1.68m), 1986.

Left: Dinah Prentice in her studio. Large works frequently have to be put together on the floor.

Left: "Doorway",
6'8" × 4'10" (2.03 × 1.47cm),
1986. A powerful response to
war in the Lebanon. The
painting shown underneath
the quilt, on the same theme,
was completed first.

Above: "Are we staying or going?", 7'2" × 9'2" (2.18 × 2.79m), 1985.

houses down in the city.

"Are we staying or going?" is a quotation from the TV series *Edge of Darkness*. It is about the sinister connection between S.D.I. and sci-fi. "Going where?" asks the blinkered diplomat of the powerful industrial cynics, who know that the earth will be uninhabitable if science and technology are allowed to advance unfettered by human imperatives.

When I paint on quilts, I don't feel satisfied because it doesn't seem finished. With painting I feel it is never entirely finished, because you can always move an edge. But in sewing you can't move an edge. I like that. I think I'm interested in edges, because if you get the edge right you can make the "space" 35 miles (56 km) or two inches (5 cm) away. I'm thrilled by that ambiguity. This

only happens when I'm sewing, not when I'm painting. That's why I will go on sewing.

Quilting suits me from a feminist point of view. Quilts reflect the "fractured" nature of women's lives, both from day to day and throughout the years. The fracturing at that dead edge where one fabric stops and another starts is a mirror image of the physical quality of a woman's life. We are saying, "Our life *is* fractured": motherhood, childbirth, menopause, children leaving home. We are constantly rationalizing new sets of rules. Quilts repeat that image. They contain that. They are a poetic equivalent.

I am very touched by the tradition of quilting. In the book *The Long Winter* (the last book in the series of *Last House on the Prairie*) the mother makes a quilt for Laura

Left: The shapes of letters have always held a fascination for Dinah Prentice and have appeared in several of her quilts.

when she marries. There is a strong sense of the terrible life that they led. When the family moved further West all they took with them was the cart, the dog, the stove and the what-not. Their hardiness was unbelievable. The quilt told this story.

The question is often asked whether quilts are art or craft. I think the division remains a problem for other people, not me. It did worry me, but now I have found a dye I can paint with, I can do everything I want to do. I have resolved the question for myself. Some people feel there is no relationship between those admittedly ravishingly made traditional quilts and the sort of quilts I make. They are quite right: they are poles apart. I think wonderful stitching is wonderful, but I can't do it! I just happen to patch things together. I happen to wad and back them, because that makes them very durable.

It is my job now to make quilts so powerful that people cannot ignore them.

WENDY HOLLAND, Sydney, Australia

Wendy Holland has a diploma in art and taught for four years. She is particularly interested in the origins of fabrics and her quilts reflect her fascination with different cultures.

I have always been attracted to old, unusual materials, particularly oriental fabrics. Before I started to make quilts I studied painting. It was the decorative aspects in painting that increased my interest in decorative and applied arts. I had first seen new patchwork quilts at a huge agricultural show, but they had left a vague impression of lime and purple hexagons, stitched with endless tedium. Seeing old quilts was a revelation – it was the fabrics that initially attracted me. I liked the odd ways the materials and patterns had been used, especially where the fabrics com-

Right: "Souvenir from Cairo", 7'7" × 6'4" (2.31 ×1.92m), 1984.

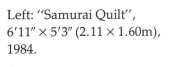

pletely confused the traditional graphic unit.

"Souvenir From Cairo" is part of a series of garment-related quilts. It suggests one of those garish, Eastern garments, brightly patched or embroidered, with different fabrics in odd places, such as underarm gussets. It also has a reference to those African drawstring trousers, with enormously wide crutches that all gather up. The pyramids on the postcard fabric (down the side) are echoed across the garment enhancing the suggestion of a bright, hot landscape.

"Samurai Quilt" is part of the same series and has the feel of a Japanese garment. It is made from a large banner depicting a Samurai warrior – the kind they hang out in the streets on children's day in Japan. I loved the areas of decoration and stylization of the warrior, his saddle, armour and so on, so I cut those out in large and small squares.

Above: ''Pale Ladies'',
7′11″ × 6′6″ (2.40 × 1.98m),
1986.

Above: "Collected Cosmic
Fragments", 6'9" × 5'9"
(2.06 × 1.76m), 1986. Japanese
materials provided the
inspiration for this quilt.

The challenge of dividing a quilt up into different areas, while still being part of a whole, appeals to me. I also like mixing cross-cultural fabrics, for example English roses and cherries with Japanese fabrics. With "The Sea Change" (not illustrated) I used Indonesian as well as Japanese fabrics, again suggesting a Japanese short jacket and Filipino puffed sleeves. There is also a Shinto shrine reference, a gateway into the Eastern Garden of Eden (another feminine symbol, along with the triangle). The lower half is made from a quilt top I printed in a traditional ocean waves pattern, which I then cut up – hence a "sea change", a quote from *The Tempest*.

The quilt "Pale Ladies" also has garment references and contains lots of pale old fabrics. The central panel is of little printed pictures of colonial American origin, pieced together. There is a repeated lady in a pale floral dress. Other fabrics include Japanese handkerchiefs printed with Japanese ladies, cut up. The diagonals on each side refer to the sticks stuck through their hair-dos. This quilt started as a traditional medallion quilt, just a vehicle for the fabrics, but it got changed along the way. The feminine symbol of the triangle is suggested here also.

"Collected Cosmic Fragments" is made from old Japanese kasuri and striped cottons (many pre-Hiroshima, which I cut as little as possible) as a gesture towards the International Year of Peace in 1986.

My quilts may not appear very Australian; there are other people using more Australian motifs and colours. However, we are very aware that we are part of Asia. But maybe I would make the same quilts in whatever part of the world I lived.

Below: Wendy Holland in her studio, concentrating on some delicate machine piecing.

LINDA MacDONALD, California, USA

I create an environmental space filled with pattern, geometric progressions and illusionary forms. My quilts are large – an imaginary window that can be stepped into – or something that one can be enveloped by. The bed-sized quilt has the advantage of a big statement or, should I say, monumental statement. Small quilts must compete with all other similar-sized wall hangings and trivialness becomes something to think about and to avoid.

My goal is to have every area of the quilt full of interest and activity. The quilt stitch that is solely functional will not do; it is not enough. Quilting provides a great opportunity to add a linear statement. It is like a pencil line-drawing over the complete image and the better it is played up the more exciting the resultant image. The

distance for viewing the actual quilting is close; the distance for viewing the whole quilt is farther away.

It may be my delight in the horror vacui *philosophy of the Victorian age, but seeing that large undecorated surface of the quilt back made me want to fill it up. I have therefore been adding simple geometric designs for the reverse side. The most unexpected result of this patterned back is how well it sets off my quilting. The quilting, totally relating to the front, becomes, on the back, an abstract line statement of its own, framed by the simple geometrics of colour. Also, it becomes a two-sided quilt. This, of course, is not new, but in the American culture of "more is better", two sides is almost always better than one.*

Left: "Salmon Ladders", 7'8" × 7'8" (2.34 × 2.34m), 1986.

Right: "Clear Palisades",
7'8″ × 7'8″ (2.34 × 2.34m),
1987.

Right: Reverse side of "Clear
Palisades".

FRAN SOIKA,
Ohio, USA

I was commissioned to do "The Nutcracker" for The Cleveland Ballet. It was raffled as a fund-raising project. These are the set designs used in The Nutcracker, *and many of the fabrics are cuttings from the costumes.*

"The Parakeet and the Mermaid" is inspired by Henri Matisse's cut-out designs.

Opposite: "The Parakeet and the Mermaid", 8'11" × 7'4" (2.72 × 2.34m), 1985.

Left: "The Nutcracker", 7'10" × 6'2" (2.39 × 1.88m), 1986. Scenes from the ballet provide the images for this quilt.

THERESE MAY, California, USA

Therese May trained as a painter and started quilting when painting proved too difficult while raising children. However, her early training proved impossible to leave completely, so her work developed to bring together both painting and quiltmaking. She has exhibited widely in the United States, and lives in San José.

I started making quilts when my kids were small, because I found it wasn't practicable to carry on painting. I felt uncomfortable having the children there while trying to paint, because it has to be the only thing I'm doing. But I couldn't stay away from being an artist for long. It was a struggle to keep on producing while the children were small. Sewing was something I could be interrupted at. That's why I started it. It was a matter of being compulsive and determined to carry on.

I started making quilts for our beds, and then baby quilts. I did squares and triangles. I didn't go by any set pattern. I cut up pieces and sewed them together. Then I started using photographic images and doing portrait quilts. For these I would project a slide on to a piece of paper. I would make a drawing, cut it into pieces and use it as a pattern. The quilts were appliquéd. Eventually my quilts stopped being for beds and started being for walls. At this point I began considering my quilts in the same frame of mind as my painting. In fact when I used photographic images, people began calling the quilts "art". I hadn't thought of them as "art" before. They were just an outgrowth of being a housewife and mother.

I worked on photographic quilts for about ten years, including large quilts with snapshot images of family and friends. In 1977 I started painting and drawing again and the imagery was fantasy-based, with animals and plants. I was influenced by the patterns in early American hooked and braided rugs, as well as by contemporary northern Californian painters such as Joan Brown and Roy Deforest, and a ceramicist, David Gilhooley, who works with animal imagery.

This led to a dramatic change. I had kept sketch books but hadn't used my paintings and drawings for my quilt work. I began incorporating them into the photographic images on the quilts. For example, I have a collection of salt and pepper shakers. "Radish Salt and Pepper Shakers" was based on a photograph of them, with other imagery added. I worked with this combination for a while, but my latest quilts have no photographic imagery at all.

I struggled with whether to return to painting, because people would say: "You really are a painter. Why don't you just paint, instead of fooling around with this fabric?" – a questionable point of view as far as the art world goes! But it was too hard to give up. I had been quilting for over ten years and had already gained a reputation. It was part of me. Painting was still part of me, but not in the same way. When I was just a painter, I was single. I was absolutely alone. It was just me. But there is something about making quilts which somehow includes everybody else.

Above: "Radish Salt and Pepper Shakers", 36″ × 50″ (91 × 127cm), 1980.

People don't have to be artists to be interested in quilting. Maybe it's the competitive spirit in the art world that adds to the differences between quilting and painting. I think quilts are accessible. Quilts put you in touch with your heritage.

Just think how people automatically think about their beds. How cosy! What could be more friendly than a quilt! Even though it's not meant to be put on a bed, you still think of snuggling up when you see a quilt. If they are in any way traditional, they contain a piece of somebody's dress, nightgown, or old shirt. They are so personal. I've been collecting fabric for years, and can recognize at least one piece of fabric that came from the past in each quilt of mine.

There were hints of fantasy images in my painting. When I was a kid I did a lot of cartooning and fun drawings. Many images come from childhood hallucinations, imagination and dreams. I am also influenced by the images used in early American folk art.

I work very automatically. I draw my images on paper. I cut the shapes out and replace the paper shapes with the fabric. I work as I go, choosing the fabric, putting on paint or adding the border. I have a fairly clear idea of where I'm going because the quilting techniques demand that, whereas when I paint I can be more spontaneous. You can change a lot more with a painting than with a quilt. As I introduce more painting into my quilts, I can work more spontaneously. It's fun to have a quilt at a finished stage and then paint on it. I've been doing this for so long that I know it's going to be OK. I trust myself, but I'm pretty conservative with the paint at the end!

I can look at a quilt as a painting and say that it needs a little more here, or something there. I visualize the colours as I go along. I go to my shelves, full of fabric, and pick something out. It's like mixing paint, but there is a difference in that you don't actually have to mix up the colour. You can see the colour already there, and it can be used as it is. It's like readymade art.

"Sawblade" was inspired by a giant sawblade I saw at a county fair one year that had a beautiful landscape painted on it. I have used a braided rug pattern rather than a landscape and a variety of fabrics for the thousands of small patches. The quilt started as a simple drawing on butcher paper. I cut the drawing to make the pattern and pinned each piece of fabric to canvas. I used a straight stitch and satin stitch around each shape, leaving a loop of thread each time I finished a small length of stitching. This created a rich, textured surface of thread. After constructing the quilt I embellished the surface with dabs of

Below: "Sawblade", 5'7" × 6'7" (1.70 × 2.01m), 1983.

Above: "Monster Quilt 2",
3'11" × 4'4" (1.19 × 1.32m),
1982.

acrylic paint. This procedure is used on all of my quilts, with slight variations.

"Monster Quilt 2" is part of a series of monster quilts. They show different shapes and sizes of creatures inspired by the ones that were hiding under my bed when I was a kid! This quilt was constructed with a variety of fabrics, such as cotton-polyester and satin, and embellished with acrylic paint. The pieces were sewn to muslin and the quilt is stuffed with batting for a soft, fluffy effect. It is made up of nine squares sewn together, but there are pieces that are appliquéd on top to look like they're floating. I can do the same thing with paint.

"Monster Quilt 4" is a continuation of the series started in 1982 and is about childhood fears, night-time visions and being at home. Each of the four monsters has teeth, but their colour and pattern make them friendly.

The centre of "Climb Every Mountain" depicts a kitchen sink with two large candlesticks at the sides. Behind the sink is a window through which we can see

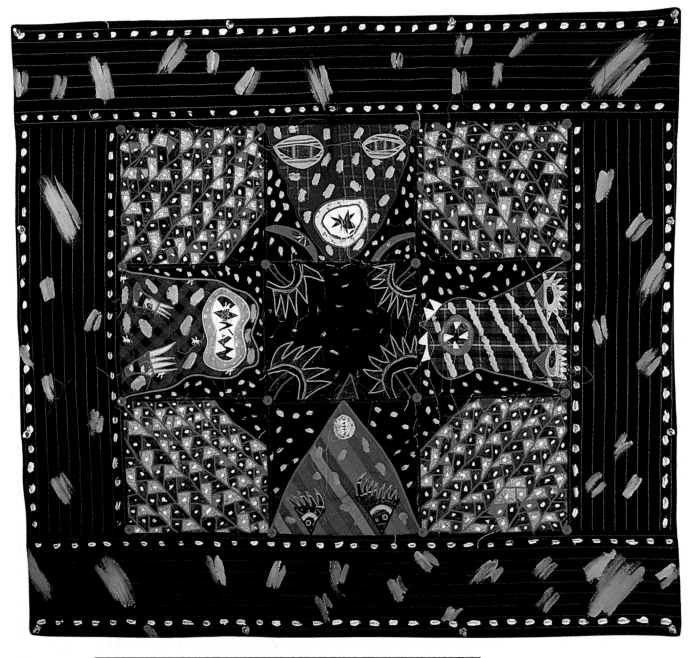

Above: "Monster Quilt 4",
4'6" × 4'11" (1.37 × 1.50m),
1985. Pieced fabric,
embellished with acrylic
paint.

Left: "Climb Every Mountain"
(detail). This uses images
symbolic of personal growth.

Above: "Fish and Chicks",
7' × 7' (2.13 × 2.13m), 1986.
Acrylic paint is once again
used as part of the work.

mountains, representing personal
growth. This is surrounded with a
patchwork of braided rug patterns
that are light in value compared to
the relatively dark colours of the
centre.

I have used various images of
fish and chickens since about
1977. I usually don't think much
about the symbolism while I'm
working, but rather I concentrate

on the fun of how the piece looks,
the delight of the shapes and the
involvement with the colours and
patterns. "Fish and Chicks" is the
beginning of a renewal, or new
cycle in my work. A more apt title
might be "Fish and Chicks and
Tulips and Shamrocks and a
Christmas Tree"! For me, fish represent the deepest feelings. Fish
swimming around under the

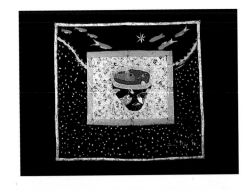

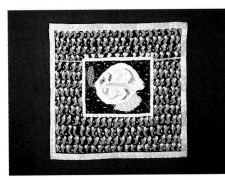

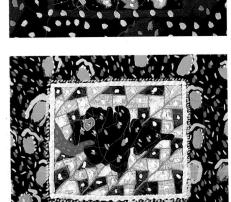

Top pair. Left: ''Imperfect Quilt 1: Fish Cup'', 41″ × 45″ (104 × 114cm), 1986. Right: ''Imperfect Quilt 2: Love-Weed-Bird'' (detail).

Second pair. Left: ''Imperfect Quilt 3: Tulip'', 41″ × 45″ (104 × 114cm), 1986. Right: ''Imperfect Quilt 4: Anthurium'' (detail).

Third pair. Left: ''Imperfect Quilt 6: Connecting Animals'', 41″ × 45″ (104 × 114cm), 1986. Right: ''Imperfect Quilt 7: Bubbling Fish'', 29″ × 29″ (74 × 74cm), 1986.

Fourth pair. Left: ''Imperfect Quilt 8: Patty-Fish'' (detail). Right: ''Imperfect Quilt 9: Pancake-Fish'', 29″ × 29″ (74 × 74cm), 1986.

Bottom pair. Left: ''Imperfect Quilt 10: Oakleaf-Fish'' (detail). Right: ''Imperfect Quilt 11: Tropical Fish'', 29″ × 29″ (74 × 74cm), 1986.

Top: "Imperfect Quilt 13: Braided Fish", 29" × 29" (74 × 74cm), 1986.

Second: "Imperfect Quilt 15: Stripped Fish" (detail).

Third: "Imperfect Quilt 17: Sweet-Fish", 29" × 29" (74 × 74cm), 1986.

Fourth: "Imperfect Quilt 18: Extending Fish" (detail).

Bottom left: "Imperfect Quilt 19: Box-Fish", 29" × 29" (74 × 74cm), 1986.

Bottom right: "Imperfect Quilt 20: Lobster Fish" (detail).

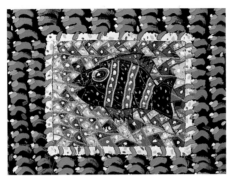

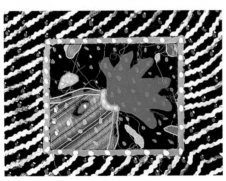

water in the ocean are like deep emotions and I suppose each quilt of a fish exposes one of these feelings. Uncovering and expressing is like healing. Chicks represent rebirth, tulips are happiness and childhood, shamrocks are for St Patrick and the Trinity, and the Christmas tree is for Christ, while the braided rug patterns are for home.

The "Imperfect Quilts" represent another new beginning. My previous work has been very successful and satisfying but I actually felt intimidated by my own accomplishment and was hesitant to begin anew for fear that I would fall flat on my face. I decided to cast fear aside and accept whatever came out and that the quilts did not have to measure up to anything; they did not have to be perfect. The important thing was to keep them going.

Before I started painting again, I exhibited in many shows that were craft-orientated, but they were somehow saying that this is really art, even though we're using a craft medium. I found that, even though people thought the world of my quilts, working in fabric wasn't quite acceptable. Now, for me, this view has changed. It could be because I paint as well as quilt and exhibit both together. A lot of the change has taken place within me. I am more confident about my work and I've been very lucky to have gained so much support.

HELEN BITAR, Oregon, USA

"The Coming of Magic" was inspired by Mount St Helens erupting in a magical way. The earth is speaking to us and we must awaken and listen.

Above: "The Coming of Magic", 4'11" × 6'5" (1.50 × 1.96m), 1982. This is a quilt which is full of meaning and mystical symbolism. The vivid reds, repeated in many of the images, also represent the fire of the volcano, while the crazed pattern on the background fabric gives an impression of the disturbed earth. Most of the work is done in appliqué.

JANE POWELL,
Shropshire, England

The most appealing part of quiltmaking was the idea of producing something lasting and functional.

I print and dye my own fabrics. I use appliqué and painting rather than patchwork, which I find restricting. I like to have the freedom to change my design ideas as I go along.

One of the things that I find most interesting is exploiting the textural qualities of traditional hand quilting, which is well worth the time involved. It gives my work some sort of shape, form and substance.

Below: "Fresco", 1984. The technique of spray painting features in this wall hanging.

Left: "Reflection", 1984.
Potato printing and shadow
quilting combine to produce a
very soft effect here.

JUDY MATHIESON, California, USA

I usually see a quilt as a problem-solving situation. With "Masquerade" it was to create a piece to remind me of my collaboration with Betye Saar on the "Artist and the Quilt" project, which combined the work of various contemporary artists with quilters. It formed a travelling exhibition and a book. We had cooperated to create a quilt called "Fantasies". Her work is normally with found objects arranged in collage. In my "Masquerade", I tried to learn from her way of working but interpret similar elements in my own way.

I can see that some of the ideas I

Below: "Masquerade", 4'4" × 4'4" (1.32 × 1.32m), 1983.

absorbed from Betye crept into "Migration". The quilt is the fourth in a series based on lattice or window designs. Working with a series opens up the process of creativity for me. In what other way can I use the same ideas? The fabric itself inspired the quilt. Two different printed batik fabrics were cut up and combined to create this "scene". A full-size cut-out of the lattice was made from paper. The fabric was first of all held behind the empty spaces, then different parts of the design were cut and rearranged behind the holes. After a new scene was created, the lattice was pieced. In a few places birds and clouds were appliquéd to facilitate the organization of the scene. The most creative part of this whole piece for me was the "Goose Chase" border, which starts very vaguely and then gets bolder and eventually turns into birds which fly back into the picture.

Left: "Migration". A traditional border is incorporated into the pictorial imagery.

JENNIFER KINGSTON, Dublin, Ireland

Jennifer Kingston's quilts have a strong narrative theme, often inspired by poetry, and she has developed her own particular technique for translating her ideas into fabric. She has exhibited in Ireland, England, the USA and Canada.

When I made my first quilt around 1970 I didn't know anybody else in the world making quilts. I just had scraps which I cut up into squares and sewed together, but I must have heard about patchwork somewhere. When I had finished it, I realized that using the colours had given me great satisfaction, and I had enjoyed making it. I've never actually made a traditional quilt.

Appliqué appealed to me and my quilts developed from this technique. Being an illustrator it seemed natural to me to make pictures rather than sew squares together. I am happiest illustrating and a number of my quilts are really illustrations.

"The Zodiac and 4 Elements" quilt was a terrific break-through for me because I went to a workshop given by Linda Straw from England in 1982. She taught me a technique of drawing designs on to cloth and transposing them on to the fabrics. There is none of this cutting out, sewing around and turning in, which makes the fabric so stiff and unnatural.

This technique of appliqué is very free. I find the spontaneity it offers most satisfying, because the making of a quilt itself is so laborious. I feel that I can draw with the machine. I lower the pressure foot and the feed-dogs so the needle just goes up and down, and I move the fabric. For me it's almost as fast as a pencil. The only problem is that you can't make mistakes! If you had to undo a line of very fine satin stitch you'd spend a thousand hours over it.

I consider "The Zodiac and 4 Elements" my most important quilt. It was a break-through and the design was just what I wanted. It works both as a wall hanging and as a bed quilt. Yet behind the finished "Zodiac", there are the beginnings of a whole lot of other quilts. "Zodiac" started off by being made up of four large squares, depicting the elements. Instead of being sensible and working out the whole design fully on paper, I made the pieces up, finished, quilted and then put them all together. It didn't work!

I finally got "Zodiac" right. Then I had to make something for another exhibition. I made "In the Oceans Cool and Deep" (a line from Milton). This one is very much influenced by Japanese prints, or rather the memory of a Japanese print. The curl of the waves and the surf are part of the memory. With this quilt, I did no drawing out beforehand because I had the centre panel already (an abandoned part of the "Zodiac" quilt) and it grew from there. To do the sea I used the same technique as before. I've developed my own techniques in my own personal style. This heavy machine quilting is uniquely mine.

I made "The Ark in the Eye of the Storm" for an exhibition called "Noah's Ark" and I only had about six weeks to make it. What a

Opposite: ''The Zodiac and 4
Elements'', 4'4" × 4'4"
(1.32 × 1.32m), 1983.

Right: Drawing of ''The Ark in
the Eye of the Storm''.

Below: ''The Ark in the Eye of
the Storm'', 5'6" × 5'6"
(1.68 × 1.68m), 1984.

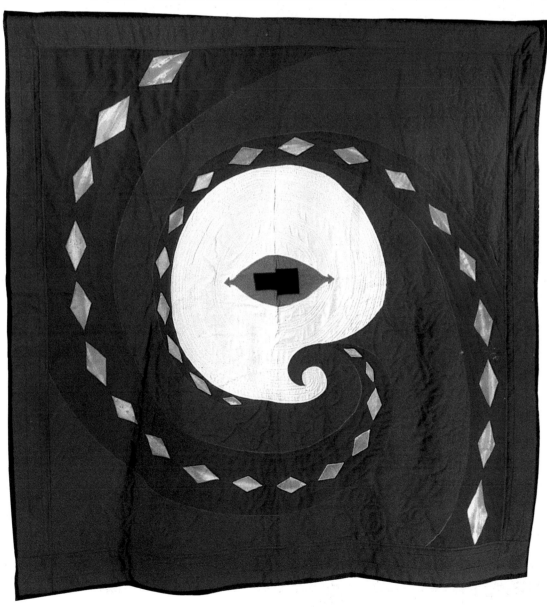

hassle! I made waves until the cows came home and again I ended up with the beginnings of four other quilts! I started with a circle and the boat, with waves advancing on it. I thought this would build up to a huge crescendo, so that the arc would be sitting on top of a great fluff of waves. It didn't work! The waves were too small and it looked fiddly. I always want to get energy into my quilts and my thoughts have great energy, but I couldn't express the energy of the waves. It worked on paper, it worked in my mind, and I thought it would work in the quilt!

So I had to start it again. Having put several weeks' work into these little waves, time was now running out, so I decided to do one big wave straight on to the fabric. With an idea as concise and lim-

ited as the "Eye of the Storm", I had a very strong image of how it should be. The "Zodiac" quilt was less frustrating as I did not have such a definite preconceived idea about it.

In my quilts I want to make the cloth do what I feel it can do. I never find fabric a restriction. It has a tactile quality that nothing else has. To me it's a form of sculpture. One of the great things about all patchwork is its wraparoundness. It connects with the mother in me, the feeling of wanting to protect the baby and the family. I think that's why women make quilts. Women are predominantly practical people and we want what we make to be usable. I'm very hooked on quilts, but it's a love-hate relationship because I have such a battle with them. Even if the design fails, it's always

Left: "Coral Reef", 5'6" × 5'8" (1.68 × 1.73m), 1985.

a good bed-cover.

"Coral Reef" is one of the "Noah's Ark" cast-offs. The waves became too fussy and were not threatening or engulfing. So I created "Coral Reef". It's a happy sort of a quilt. The dots are stuck on and sewn across, so that the edges might lift and be free.

In April 1986 I attended a workshop on dye-painting given by Linda Brassington. This added another dimension to what I could do with fabric. I started dye-painting the base fabric and building up the pictorial image with strips, tiny scraps and various-sized squares. After sticking on the applied fabric, I cover the whole thing with coloured net or transparent materials, sewing everything with transparent thread.

"Fuchsia in Marley Park" was created with this technique, using net extensively. "November on my Windowsill" has no dye-painting on the base fabric. The colour is built up with very many layers of patterned and plain transparent materials.

Right: "Fuchsia in Marley Park", 36″ × 30″ (91 × 76cm), 1987. Dye-painted fabric and net give the impression of a watercolour painting.

I start many of my quilts with a line of poetry, or a title. I read poetry a lot, and certain poems will trigger off my imagination. Many are poems I have read as a child, that I have chewed over in my subconscious over the years. At the moment it is colour that excites me, and trees and forests are my main subjects.

Above: "November on my Windowsill", 33″ × 34″ (84 × 86cm), 1986. Layers of transparent materials create the image in this quilt, an entirely original technique.

VICKI JOHNSON, California, USA

Above: "A Bright Winter Day in Mendocino", 6'9" × 5'4" (2.06 × 1.63m), 1984. Traditional squares, triangles and strips blend with the scenic landscape of rocks, ocean, houses and sky, and the picture merges with the border. Quilting lines skilfully form the waves in the foreground. This quilt shows that many different techniques can be used in the same work to achieve a specific effect.

I start with an idea of something I wish to express and a visual concept of how to go about it. I do a very simple thumbnail drawing and allow the idea to grow – I dwell on it in odd moments, perhaps when I'm riding in the car, or going to sleep.

I begin with a piece of muslin and I paint the landscape. I work over this with appliqué and then do the surrounding piecing. I use a great many techniques – whatever seems to be the best way to achieve the desired design – but all of these must produce a functional quilt, one that can be used on a bed. This means all are washable, even though most of mine are hung on the wall. I think this is an important point, because it ensures that the work is strong and therefore more permanent. I like the fact that quilts can be works of art which are also functional.

The quilt "A Bright Winter Day in Mendocino" is an expression of the sky along the ocean, of the openness and airiness, with the clouds flowing colour and light. Part of this was achieved by breaking out of the surrounding border.

I often use the reverse side of fabrics because the colours are more muted and blend with the painted part better. Integrating the painting and fabric is important. I want them to flow together.

MARIEL CLARMONT,
Paris, France

My work combines the varied techniques of patchwork to form wall hangings. I work in raw silk encrusted with a mosaic of coloured fabrics, entirely sewn and quilted by hand, and sometimes even embroidered with glass beads. I call these pieces "artipatches". My work requires long, conceptual studies, rough sketches and diagrams and then a related series of drawings.

The "artipatches" connect movement created in relief with the dynamics of colour, according to the rhythms inspired by Far Eastern meditation panels, such as Tibetan "tantras". It is the creation of relief that often gives the work a character that's almost hypnotic.

The difference between traditional American patchwork, whose geometrical forms and the repetition of images is almost unchangeable and purely decorative, and "artipatches" is that these are the product of a study of the expressive qualities of textiles, when freed from the constraints of tradition.

Below: "Artipatch: Mandala 10", 4'7" × 5'11" (1.40 × 1.80m), 1983.

Above: "Artipatch: Paradis
perdu I" (detail). This close-
up illustrates the neatness and
perfection of Mariel
Clarmont's hand quilting and
piecing. The selected fabrics
contrast beautifully with the
raw silk which forms the basis
of the work, while the touches
of gold add an exotic flavour
to the quilt.

SIEGRUN BOSS, Sindelfingen, West Germany

I developed my quilting technique after I saw pictures of ''white work'' and ''trapunto'' coverlets illustrated in American quilt books. It opened up the possibility of elaborating forms with extremely fine stitches and achieving a low relief with sensitive outlines, which produce contrast in light and shadow, and create with it a texture all of its own.

With this technique I have developed a series of quilts which focus in a very representational way on a variety of similar and familiar objects. Thus, I take well-known situations from everyday life and transfer them into an unexpected medium. In the example illustrated, it is knitted socks on a clothes line. I like to work with similar and comparable objects, whereby each element relates to the whole and to each other. It demands the attention and makes the viewer look a second time more carefully. This quilt is amusing and makes people smile!

Below: ''Laufend – M 305'', 36" × 42" (92 × 107cm), 1983.

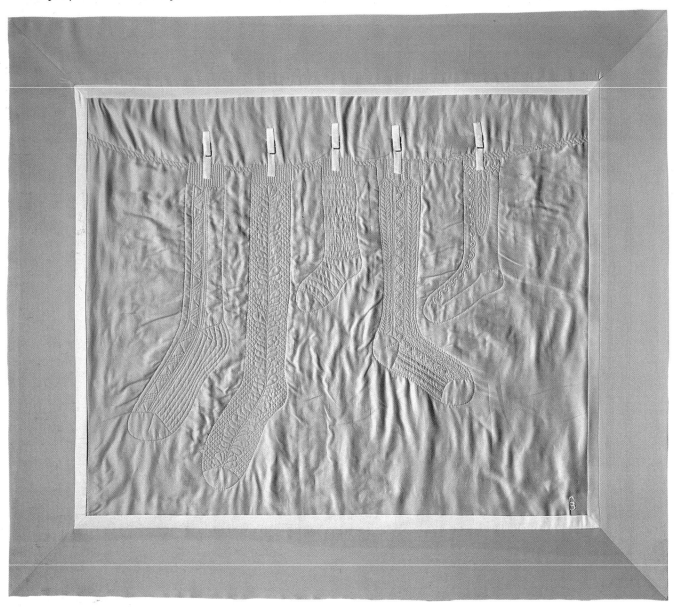

NADINE ROGERET, Le Havre, France

Nadine Rogeret runs her own quilt shop in Le Havre, where she both makes her own quilts and teaches quilting techniques to a growing number of people. She practises traditional hand-sewn techniques, maintaining the absolute necessity for technical expertise.

I began by making traditional patchwork because I wanted to acquire the techniques. I learnt from an American called Sophie Campbell, who spent time teaching patchwork in France. I believe that to execute patchwork, it is absolutely necessary to learn traditional motifs and methods. Only having accomplished this can you begin to create anything new. The process is very mathematical and it is necessary to work through these traditional motifs in order to understand them. To create a design, you must know how to construct it beforehand.

I attach great importance to a full study of technique, without which I could not create. Some quilters have started as painters, but I'm more of a technician. I want to know everything and have therefore studied all varieties of patchwork world-wide.

In appliqué you invent a design more like a painter, for instance, flowers, the countryside; it's a

Right: "Le Diamant",
4'3" × 4'3" (1.30 × 1.30m),
1984.

fluid method. Geometric patchwork rests on technique. If an idea comes to you of a geometrical motif, it requires a structure. In my opinion, something can't be "well made" unless it's technically well done. For instance, my ideas for "Le Diamant" relied upon my technique. To start with, I did a sketch and from this I made a scale drawing and then the templates. The process for "Les 5000 Triangles" and "Sunburst" was similar. I work only by hand. It takes me a long time to produce a piece of work.

I want to make patchwork for a living. I run my shop, I teach patchwork and I must sell my work. My commissions are for

Below: "Les 5000 Triangles" (detail), 7' × 7' (2.15 × 2.15m), 1979.

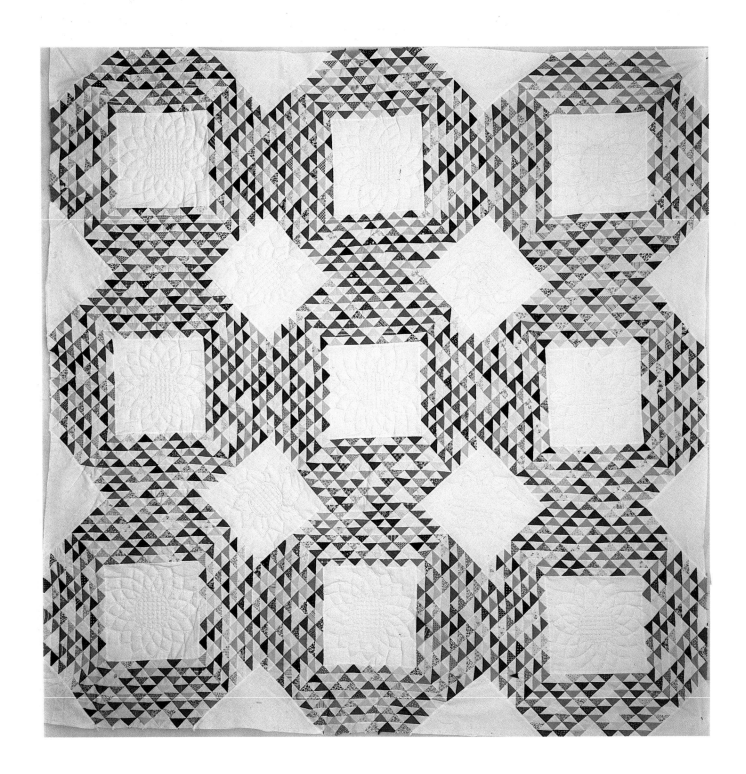

Above: Nadine Rogeret in her studio, displaying one of her quilts.

Right: ''Sunburst'', 7'11" × 7'3" (2.40 × 2.20m), 1985.

traditional quilts, but I am preparing a collection of patchwork which involves lots of technique but with contemporary design. In France, patchwork is still not very well known and therefore traditional quilts dominate, although myself and others are working towards a more varied range of quilts.

Patchwork for me brings together exactly the things that I love: the colours, the preparation, the fabric (I only use American or English cotton); it is a medium which is very pleasing to work with and gives me satisfaction.

JOS VERCAUTEREN,
Antwerp, Belgium

I became interested in three-dimensional patchwork and began to study colour, making hundreds of sketches to observe the interaction between colours, blocks and patterns. Sometimes I put traditional patterns together, then take a part of that sketch out and work with it so that a new pattern emerges by accentuating some lines or parts.

I have always worked with pure cotton fabrics. I machine the tops of my quilts but do the actual quilting by hand.

Below: "Flying Boxes",
4'2" × 4'2" (1.28 × 1.28m),
1985.

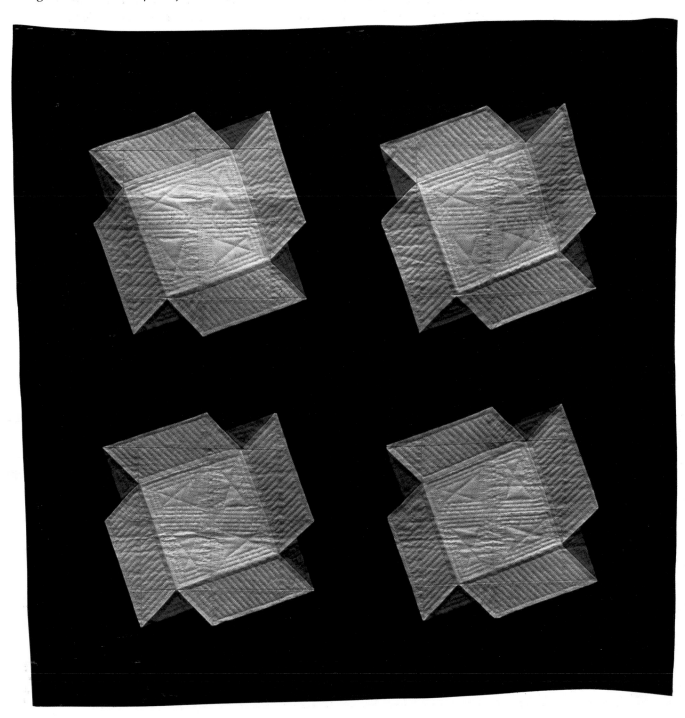

MARIE-JOSÉ MICHEL,
Rouen, France

I began by making very traditional quilts, taking classes to learn the main techniques and patterns, such as ''Log Cabin'' and ''Pineapple''. In the quilt ''March – A Quilt for all Seasons'' (part of a series), I began experimenting and it was a good exercise to employ the miscellaneous techniques I had learnt.

I now take more interest in researching and developing illustrations of, for instance, tilework and mosaics from various churches and mosques, which provide me with a rich source of inspiration. One quilt was influenced by a pavement from St Mark's Basilica in Venice, Italy. The quilt ''Allah'' (overleaf) was taken from a mosaic in a mosque at the old Islamic centre of Samarkand.

Below: ''March – A Quilt for all Seasons'', 24″ × 24″ (60 × 60cm), 1985.

Above: ''Allah'', 3'11" × 3'11"
(1.20 × 1.20m), 1985. Entirely
traditional techniques result in
a stunning design, inspired by
a mosaic in a mosque. The
blending of the colours within
the geometric pattern is
cleverly achieved and adds
interest to the overall effect.

LUCINDA GANE,
London, England

Two aspects of quiltmaking attract me particularly: the creation of something beautiful out of scraps, and the fabrication of a surface composed of shapes and colours I have chosen. I prefer to work in silk and cotton.

I either start with the colours in mind or with fabrics I already have, as with the "Silk Tie" quilt. I had accumulated a large number of silk ties and by using them I felt that I was getting closer to the traditional purpose of patchwork – to use up scraps that would otherwise be wasted. In this way I was able to incorporate a wide variety of silks, which I treated in various ways; I stripped the dye out of some, reversed others and, when the tie linings were especially attractive, I used those as well.

The pattern for the "Aztec" quilt (overleaf) had been in my mind for some time before I found the fabric I wanted. I had a clear vision of the colours used in Mexican pottery – light grey-blue, terracotta and yellow ochre. Of course the pattern is not genuinely Aztec, but the jagged, angular, asymmetrical and symmetrical shapes suggested the title.

My quilts are hand pieced, and hand and machine finished.

Below: "Silk Tie Quilt", 6'1" × 6'1" (1.85 × 1.85m), 1984.

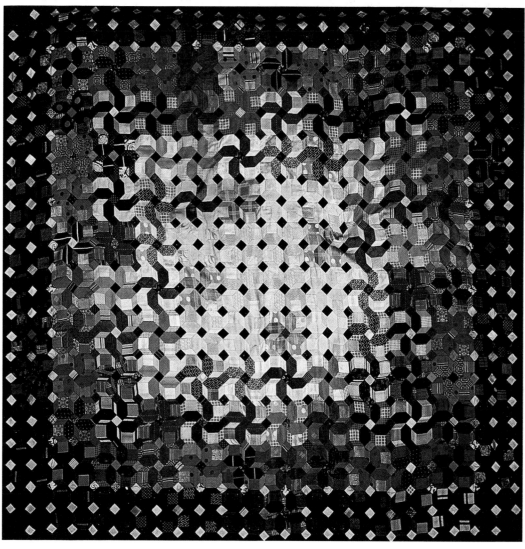

Above: ''Aztec'', 6'7" × 6'7"
(2.01 × 2.01m), 1984. Strong
shapes produce a striking
design with a Mexican tribal
feel. This quilt is hand pieced.

RUTH McDONNELL, Dublin, Ireland

Ruth McDonnell's training was in exhibition and interior design. She has always sewed and found the transition to two-dimensional patchwork a natural development. She has been making quilts since 1972. Her work has been included in exhibitions in Ireland, England and America, and she is a founder member of the Irish Patchwork Society. She works in Irish television as a production buyer.

The first time I saw a quilt was in Bloomingdale's Store in New York in 1972, where I was working as a student for six months. They were holding an exhibition of antique American quilts. I was amazed by them; the work and designs intrigued me. These quilts didn't seem opulent (unlike their surroundings!). They seemed like hard work. I was used to making things and could see the effort that had gone into them.

Armed with this new discovery when I returned to Ireland, I started to make patchwork. I wasn't aware of any tradition of patchwork in Ireland, but in talking to my grandmother I discovered that she had made them as a girl. People used to put old blankets into them for warmth. I never saw the quilts she made as they had been thrown out.

There is a story of a man who came to the Kilkenny Exhibition of Antique Irish Quilts in Dublin in 1980. He came to the door and then turned around. He just could not bear to go in. The quilts reminded him of times past and of being poor. Now quilts are collectors' items, but for others they are reminders of hard times.

There were no books on quilting or patchwork in Ireland when I started, so I taught myself from memory and from the sketches I had made in America. At first I didn't understand what held a quilt together – this was before the arrival of wadding and quilting threads. Mind you, my first attempts were so awful I threw them away. It takes a long time to get them right.

In my first quilts the designs were traditional. I made a few black and white ones. Working in black and white is interesting and visually satisfying. You are concerned only with pattern, texture and fabrics; there isn't the problem of "Does this yellow go with this pink?"

Starting my own designs probably happened by accident. "Flying Geese" was a slight departure from a traditional design. Some traditional quilts include a deliberate mistake in the design so as not to compete with God, and this to my mind is the best excuse for making a mistake that any quiltmaker can have! But very often quilts are "perfect" and I find that boring. I didn't want to compete with God! I am well aware that there is nothing original, but if you can put your own stamp on your work, that's good enough. It took me a long time to gain enough confidence to do this myself. With "Flying Geese" I thought it would be interesting to put in some solid blue triangles, the way that birds fly in triangular formation. I wanted to emphasize firstly the pattern and then the movement. The decision came while I was making it.

I work mainly from sketches of

Left: "Flying Geese", 7'2" × 5'7" (2.19 × 1.69m), 1979. The dark-blue triangles add emphasis to this traditional design, and give a feeling of movement.

ideas, interests, feelings – even the weather! I rarely plan a quilt exactly. I like and look forward to the element of chance, of a possibility of change mid-quilt. It is more exciting, too, as you have a sense of a new discovery while halfway through a piece. Colour, for instance, might be left to chance. I grow nerine lilies, which are bright pink, and at the time that I was making a quilt called "Lily and Leaves" my lilies came into bloom. With this in mind I then discovered a really shocking pink material. I put it in and it worked! If I hadn't, the design would have turned out in autumnal colours, but for me the pink was a great improvement.

It seems more efficient to plan and sometimes I wish I could, but I am faced with who I am. My life has never been that way. I work in television, where everyone's opinions and suggestions are considered before a decision is made, but in my patchwork no committee meeting is called. I make every decision and see the thing through from start to finish.

I hand appliquéd and quilted "Herbaceous Border". I was given some dyed cotton by a friend, as I haven't got round to dyeing my own fabric yet (perhaps because I like the tradition of using what's there). The cream fabric is calico. This wall hanging started with the material. I was doing a garden

Above: "Herbaceous Border 2", 4' × 4'4" (1.22 × 1.33m), 1984.

series at the time and was thinking about my own garden. It's much easier to work in fabric gardens than in real ones! I quilt instead of gardening; it's quicker and you don't have to wear Wellingtons. I like the strong, bold shape of "Herbaceous Border"; it reminds me of the rigidity with which "proper" gardens are kept (I will never have a proper garden!). I think it's good to make quilts which mirror or echo some areas of your own life.

For "Walled Flowers", which is a wall hanging, I was looking at brick walls around Dublin. There are Georgian squares of houses built in red brick and streets of houses built of warm grey tones. I put flowers in. Walls always seem to be so strong, but even so, flowers grow in them.

The pleated squares of "Beach 1 and 2" were made in Irish linen, which I did not piece but used as a length of fabric. I pleated it and sprayed in between each pleat with aquamarine dye. I made it more intense by spraying darker colour at one end and a lighter colour at the other, giving a

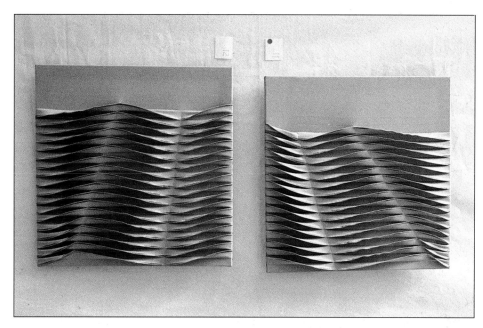

Opposite: ''Walled Flowers 2'', 51″ × 37″ (130 × 94cm), 1985.

Above right: ''Beach 1 and 2'', 24″ × 24″ (61 × 61cm). Inspired by the ripples in wet sand, as in the photograph above.

shadowy effect. I edged the pleats with a graded thread of the same colour. I used to spend summers as a child at the seaside and I know the feeling of walking with the ridges of sand under your feet. ''Beach 1 and 2'' reminds me of that texture.

Cotton is the fabric I use most because of the range of colours. It is also pleasant to iron! I have worked with a very heavy linen, too, which comes in good strong colours. If I see a nice piece of linen I buy it (and very often put it in a paper bag and lose it!). I remember all the fabrics that I have. Very often I root through every box and bag because I know I have a piece of yellow some-where.

I like to experiment with differ-ent techniques. I tend to do this on my own, but I go to workshops when I can for the sheer discipline and hopefully some new ideas come out of them as well. The idea for ''Sunny Afternoon'' struck me when we were fraying fabric. Instead of using solid coloured material, I painted it. This in-volved cutting up strips of fabric, crunching them up one at a time

into a ball, putting them in the back pocket of my tightest jeans and sitting on them. When they were taken out they were full of creases going in all directions, so then it was just a matter of paint-ing all those vein-like creases, giving a kind of marbled effect. The fringing in the rectangle was spray-dyed pink.

''Patterned Piece'' was made of cream silk with cotton fringing. The textured markings were added with fabric crayon, some of them emphasized with satin stitching of graded coloured threads. Some of the squares have satin-stitched markings.

I've seen quilts in exhibitions where the colours were lovely, the designs were gorgeous but the execution was just awful, and that bothers me. It is the combination of the technique, the design and the colours, the balance of these three elements, that is the most important part of making a quilt. I enjoy quilts and get a buzz from making them. The social side to patchwork societies and groups has always been most worthwhile. All this from a day's shopping in Bloomingdale's!

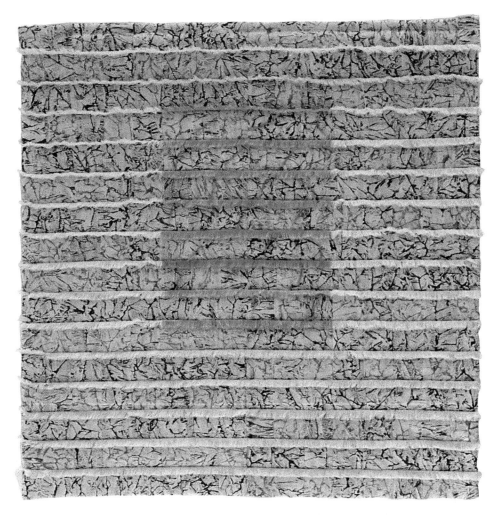

Left: "Sunny Afternoon",
37" × 37" (94 × 94cm).

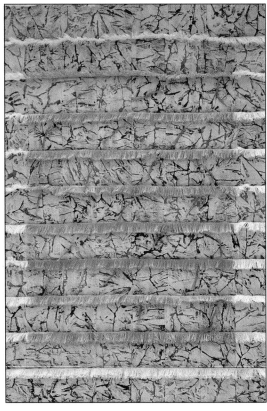

Left: Detail of "Sunny
Afternoon" showing the
material, which was first
crumpled and then painted
along the creases. The pink
fringing was spray-dyed.

Opposite: "Patterned Piece",
38" × 29½" (96 × 75cm). Fabric
crayon emphasized with satin
stitching adds the colour.

NADINE RUSÉ, Malakoff, France

I create a "super-real" world in textiles, using photographic images and bold colours on a large scale, with more than a touch of humour! The basis of the work is the creation of a different reality, without people, by giving life to the objects, the form of which is influenced by Mondrian.

In order to achieve the desired effect, I play with different materials and techniques: materials that are matt or glossy, smooth or textured; techniques that are by hand or machine, appliquéd or embroidered.

Below: "Le Store", 5'7" × 7'3" (1.70 × 2.22m), 1985. The techniques of quilting are employed here to create a new reality.

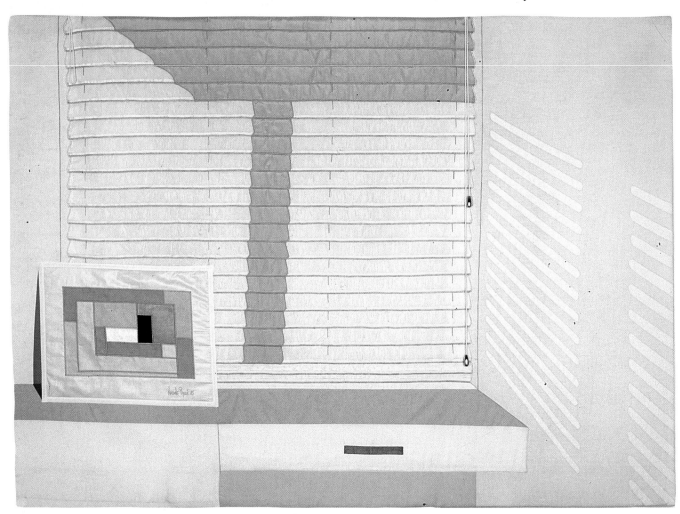

Opposite: "Le Café de la Bastille", 4'7" × 3'3" (1.40 × 1m).

CAFÉ de la BASTILLE
téléphone
BILLARD
RICARD
NADINE RUSÉ 1982

JO BUDD, East Anglia, England

My initial involvement with large-scale sewn textiles was through the patchwork quilt. Although I do not consider myself a quiltmaker in the traditional sense, both the craftsmanship of the sewing and aesthetic considerations of colour and form are of as much importance to me as they have always been to the quiltmaker. Being trained as a painter, however, meant that my interests lay more with using cloth pictorially than with the reiteration or extension of already infinitely used, though

Left: "Boatyard with Cranes", 8' × 5'4" (2.44 × 1.63m), 1981.

undoubtedly infinitely re-usable, traditional designs.

My working methods are constantly changing depending on the demands of a particular subject, as do the types of subject I use according to the discovery of new techniques. After experimenting with pre-dyed cloth, pieced together and stretched over a frame to give a flat surface (see "Boatyard with Cranes"), I became more interested in the textural qualities of the cloth itself, combining "pieced" sewing with a collage type of technique which allowed frayed edges of cloth to show (see "Gasometer"). I now dye my own fabrics because of the increased subtlety and variation of colour this offers within each individual piece of cloth. Rather than trying to eliminate shadows from the picture surface, I now use them as an element of line by placing seams on the outside of the work. The use of irregular frayed edges also gives emphasis to the nature of the cloth itself (see "Snow, Sun, Shadow").

The tactile qualities of cloth, the wealth of techniques it offers in both two and three dimensions, and its freedom from the weight of art history, all make it an appealing medium to me. Although dealing with the traditional painter's concerns of colour, shape and light, I still have a strong affinity with the less vaunted, but equally valid, art form: the quilt.

Right: "Gasometer",
6'4" × 3'6" (1.93 × 1.07m),
1983.

GLOSSARY

Amish quilts	The Amish people settled in the north-eastern states of America around 1725. The quilts they make are renowned for their strong use of colour and bold geometric designs.
Appliqué	The sewing of small pieces of fabric on to a larger background material. This can be done either by hand, turning the edges under, or by machine, which seals the edges with the satin stitch (close zig-zag stitching).
Backing	The material used for the back of the quilt. Sometimes this is also a piece of patchwork.
Batting	Otherwise known as wadding, it is the filling placed between the quilt top and the back. Nowadays it is usually polyester, but it can be cotton fibre. Wool blankets were frequently used in the past.
Quilt block	A quilt block is made up by sewing geometric pieces of fabric together to create an overall design, in the form of a square (sometimes a rectangle). When the blocks are completed they are sewn together to form the quilt top. There are hundreds of different quilt block patterns.
Crazy quilt	The quilt top is formed by sewing irregular shapes of fabric together.
Enlarging	The enlarging of the design to the size of the actual quilt to form the pattern pieces.
Frames	A quilt frame or hoop is used to hold the quilt taut, enabling the three layers to be quilted.
Hand piecing	The fabric is turned under and tacked on to paper templates. The pieces of fabric are then joined together (with the paper templates still in place) using fine hand sewing. The paper pieces are taken out when the quilt top is completed.
Hexagons	Fabric hexagons of equal size are sewn together into a honeycomb pattern that forms the quilt top. An old traditional way of making a quilt top, creating patterns such as Grandmother's Flower Garden.
Lattice strips	Strips of material used between the quilt blocks when constructing the quilt top.
Log Cabin	A traditional quilt block pattern, derived from the way log cabins are constructed.
Olfa cutter	An industrial pattern cutter.
Piecing	The method used to join different fabric pieces together. This is either by machine sewing or by hand sewing.

Quilting	The stitching used to join the three layers (top, wadding and back) of a quilt together. The quilting lines form an intricate pattern and are an integral part of the quilt. Both hand and machine quilting feature in contemporary work.
Seminole piecing	Strips of fabric sewn together, then cut up, re-arranged and re-sewn together to form complex geometric patterns.
Strip piecing	Strips of fabric sewn together, usually by machine.
Template	The master pattern piece. The quilter draws round this on to the fabric, so that the same shape can be accurately cut out again and again.
Wadding	See batting.

ACKNOWLEDGMENTS

The publishers would like to thank the following for permission to reproduce their photographs: John Coles 34 above, 60, 61, 62, 64, 65, 74; Paul Hartland 25; J. Hyde 71, 151; Jennie Jones, Inc. 110; B. Jarret 150; Lacombe 133; Don Nicholson 29 above and below, 30 above and below, 40, 41, 42, 43 above, 44 top, 45 below, 99, 100 above and below, 101; Albert Roosenburg 26; J. Six 132; Ian Tudor front cover, 105; Victoria and Albert Museum 96.

INDEX